Reflecting Children's Lives

Other Redleaf Press Books by Deb Curtis and Margie Carter

The Art of Awareness: How Observation Can Transform Your Teaching,
  second edition

Designs for Living and Learning: Transforming Early Childhood Environments,
  second edition

Learning Together with Young Children: A Curriculum Framework for
  Reflective Teachers

Training Teachers: A Harvest of Theory and Practice

The Visionary Director: A Handbook for Dreaming, Organizing,
  and Improvising in Your Center, second edition

with Debbie Lebo and Wendy C. M. Cividanes

Reflecting in Communities of Practice: A Workbook for Early Childhood
  Educators

Reflecting Children's Lives

A Handbook for Planning Your Child-Centered Curriculum

Second Edition

Deb Curtis and Margie Carter

Redleaf Press®
www.redleafpress.org
800-423-8309

Published by Redleaf Press
10 Yorkton Court
St. Paul, MN 55117
www.redleafpress.org

First edition published 1996. Second edition 2011.
Cover design by Jim Handrigan
Cover photograph by LaTisha Flowers
Interior typeset in ITC Legacy and designed by Erin Kirk New
Interior photographs provided by Deb Curtis and Margie Carter in cooperation
    with the organizations acknowledged on page xiii except photograph on page
    324, provided by Gwen Hunter
Illustrations by Claire Schipke
Printed in the United States of America

"As Human as They Can Be" by Tom Hunter was originally recorded on *As Human as They Can Be* DVD, © 2008 by the Song Growing Company. Lyrics reprinted with permission of the Song Growing Company, Bellingham, WA; www.tomhunter.com.

"Name Writing Samples" by Evelyn Lieberman was originally published in *Name Writing and the Preschool Child*, © 1985. Graphic reprinted with permission of Evelyn Lieberman.

"Worthy of Our Children" by Tom Hunter was originally recorded on *Bits & Pieces*, © 1990 by the Song Growing Company. Lyrics reprinted with permission of the Song Growing Company, Bellingham, WA; www.tomhunter.com.

Library of Congress Cataloging-in-Publication Data
Curtis, Deb.
    Reflecting children's lives : a handbook for planning your child-centered
  curriculum / Deb Curtis and Margie Carter. — 2nd ed.
        p. cm.
    Includes bibliographical references.
    ISBN 978-1-60554-039-9 (alk. paper)
    1. Early childhood education—Curricula. 2. Curriculum planning.
  3. Classroom environment.   I. Carter, Margie. II. Title.
  LB1139.4.C88 2011
  375'.001—dc22
                                                                    2010039713

Printed on acid-free paper
                                                                    U15-03

We dedicate this book to Elizabeth Jones, who has made a tremendous contribution to our thinking and practice and the advancement of our profession. Betty keeps us observing, talking, reexamining, writing, and, of course, playing. We take inspiration from who she is and what she does. With gratitude, we follow in her path.

And we dedicate this book to Marian Wright Edelman, a prophet for our time and a remarkably fierce guardian of childhood. Though we don't know her personally, she inspires us to take risks and fight for what we know to be true. When we are tired or discouraged, her work both humbles and rejuvenates us.

Finally, with deep appreciation, this book is dedicated to our sons, Casey and Peter, who deepened our understanding of childhood and fueled our passion to preserve this precious time of life.

Contents

Chapter 3 Guiding Children's Play and Learning 73

Chapter 4 Putting the Child Back in DAP 99

Chapter 5 Redefining Curriculum Themes 125

Chapter 6 Putting Academic Learning in Its Place 179

Acknowledgments

Many people have contributed to this book, directly and indirectly. Thanks to Jim Greenman, who first put the phrase "creating places for childhood" in our heads. We appreciate the wonderful contributions of stories from Christina Aubel, Laurie S. Cornelius, Sarah A. Felstiner, Evelyn Lieberman, Kelly Matthews, Kristie L. Norwood, Ann Pelo, Rukia Monique Rogers, and Ezra Stoker-Graham. Tom Hunter's wonderful song lyrics always help us make our ideas more vivid. Across the United States, Canada, and New Zealand, early childhood centers have opened their doors to us and generously gifted us with photos. For this book, we are especially grateful to the following: LaTisha Flowers for the cover photo; our New Zealand Colleagues at Browns Bay, Magic Garden, Tots Corner, and Sophia's Preschool; our Australian colleagues at Earlwood Children's Center; and our Canadian colleagues at London Bridge Child Care Services. We are grateful for the generosity of our U.S. colleagues at the Burlington Little School; Children First; the Children's Studio; Hilltop Children's Center; Refugee and Immigrant Family Center and Creekside Southwest Early Learning (SWEL), chapters of Sound Child Care Solutions; Stepping Stones; United Way Bright Beginnings YWCA Field Center; Destiny Village; and San Jacinto Child Development Center. We give special thanks to Peg Callaghan, Wendy Cividanes, Nancy Gerber, Jeanne Hunt, Debbie Lebo, and Kelly Ramsey.

Working with the editorial and production team at Redleaf Press is a writer's dream. They sharpen our thinking, writing, and aesthetic eye. Special thanks to David Heath and Carla Valadez and to illustrator Claire Schipke.

Our families and friends have come to expect our disappearance when we have a book project under way. As usual, they provided us with the needed space and focus, good meals, walks, laughs, and reminders that they, too, want to be in the circle of guardians for the precious time of life called childhood.

Introduction

Since the first edition of this book was published in 1996, the field of early care and education has entered a new era. An avalanche of research has put early childhood on the map as a prime time for learning. This new knowledge is both exciting and unsettling, and it begs some big questions. If you believe a child's mind is a terrible thing to waste, how does this belief inform your teaching approach? Child care providers, teachers, administrators, and teacher educators are scrambling to keep up with all the new standards and competing ideas about how they should do their jobs. Educational reform is on such a fast track that it's difficult to get one's bearings. With our second edition of *Reflecting Children's Lives,* we hope to get you grounded *and* excited as you set about navigating this new research to plan your curriculum for young children.

When we wrote the first edition of this book, we were inspired by Jim Greenman's call to create places for the one childhood our children will have. Jim was speaking about the growing majority of very young children who spend an estimated twelve thousand hours—from birth until they enter school—not with their families or in their neighborhoods, but in programs centered around schedules, health and risk management, and school readiness agendas. Our dismay over this reality led us to the working title for this book: "Guardians of Childhood." We wanted teachers, parents, and society as a whole to protect this precious time of life, to honor childhood, and to respect children's insatiable appetite for joyful learning. More than a decade later, we still want those things for children, but new times and deeper understandings have expanded our call to action.

Research on brain development, statistics on school failure, and the needs of a global economy have led parents, governments, and school policy makers to press for an increasingly earlier emphasis on academic learning and success. Unfortunately, many think this means more tightly prescribed programs, quantifiable learning outcomes, and rigorous schedules for younger and younger children. Time for play has all but disappeared in kindergarten classrooms, even though the research literature confirms that learning experiences for young children should take place within existing routines and play activities. Even pre-K programs are becoming academic pressure cookers with achievement outcomes driving how children spend their time—little of which is free, let alone outdoors.

Standards and assessment tools may be well intentioned in their demand for accountability, but we suspect those who develop them are not totally familiar with the daily realities of planning for young children. For teachers who want to stay child centered, the challenge is

- to make the standard teaching and documentation requirements relevant to the real work of planning for children's development and learning;

- to focus on children's competencies, not just their deficits;

- to see children as members of a family, culture, and community, and to draw on the strengths and "funds of knowledge" they bring through the door;

- to tend to the quality of children's understandings, not just the quantity of check marks in their assessments of "readiness"; and

- to weave content learning into the natural rhythm of children's play and pursuits.

Teaching and Learning

Our dear friend Tom Hunter sang, "This world is changing so fast we can't see what's coming before it's arrived. To think passing tests will get our kids ready is a gamble we take with their lives" (Hunter 2008). If you see the work of educating young children as only preparing for the future, you are in danger of overlooking who children really are— the truths they speak, the lessons they offer you, and the gift they are to your humanity. When you take up the task of "preparing" children, what picture of the future do you have in mind? If you view the job of teaching as primarily preparing children for the job market, what do you envision those jobs to be? Does your picture acknowledge that most of the jobs children will apply for as adults, along with the technologies they will use, haven't yet been invented?

Our children's future will require them to solve problems that haven't yet been identified, even as they address the somewhat predictable problems of a planet in danger of dying. At the same time, technology will connect them as global citizens to unlimited information, including instructions for everything and stunning examples of ingenuity and innovation. With this as a sketchy picture of the future, what do children really need from us? How can we teach with integrity and craft our work?

As an early childhood educator, you must continually look forward and look back, even as you stay focused on the real children in front of you and the context of their lives. The research literature provides both dismaying and exciting news. The data on the disparity between children in poverty and those in middle-class families continues to highlight the country's history of racism and economic injustice. Addressing this problem is complex and far bigger than a single teacher's job, but as educators, we want to do our very best to close this achievement gap.

Some of the early learning research particularly excites us. Neuroscience technology offers observable evidence that babies' brains function like scientists at work. Their brains make connections faster than the speed of an adult brain. How does this evidence help us better understand the growth of the achievement gap and the role teachers can play in keeping all children intellectually engaged and motivated to continue to learn? This question has guided our considerations as we've revised this book in 2010. As teacher-educators and students of the learning process ourselves, we've continued to reflect, learn from others, and advance our thinking. We now see a more active role for teachers as facilitators, guides, and coaches for children's learning. With further insights from Lev Vygotsky's theories of social constructivism, we understand that the notion of "child-centered" should be reframed as "children-centered." Teachers work with groups of children with diverse backgrounds and learning styles. Children learn different things in groups than they do on their own. Likewise, notions of "developmentally appropriate practice" should be recast to include an understanding of context and "culturally appropriate practices." Teachers must continue to translate theory into practice and use their practice to reshape teaching and learning theories.

In the first edition of this book, the writing of Lilian Katz influenced us to pay attention to dispositional learning. Today research emphasizes a similar concept—the importance of focusing on children's "approaches to learning." More recently, Katz has provoked our thinking with her distinction between academic skills and intellectual pursuits. Intellectual engagement is different from the ability to memorize, recite, and respond to flash cards or verbal cues. Intellectual engagement involves teachers asking questions they are genuinely curious about, rather than questions that test for correct answers. When children (and teachers) are intellectually engaged, they have a quest for understanding; their minds are lively, curious, puzzling things out, predicting, testing theories, and drawing conclusions, including who and what is worth learning about. On the other hand, focusing on academics usually involves exercises and work sheets to teach discrete bits of disembedded information that typically have little meaning for children. This is not to say that children can't or shouldn't learn academic content. To the contrary, extensive research indicates that young children have a hearty appetite for the particular learning domains of language, math, and science. This second edition of *Reflecting Children's Lives* offers a variety of ideas for teachers to take advantage of that appetite.

For curriculum planning to be relevant and reflect the needs of children, teachers should pay close attention to the children themselves and to the economic and ideological interests that compete for their childhoods. You must continue to develop yourself as a competent caregiver and teacher. Simultaneously, your task is to become an advocate—a strong voice and activist on behalf of children and what they and you deserve. Getting better at what you do involves taking a close look at yourself. It means making changes, taking risks, and building systems for collaboration and support. Like children, teachers and caregivers are engaged in a developmental process and construct understandings relevant for their own contexts. You will find stories to that effect at the end of each chapter in this book. Some of these stories are new contributions to this second edition of *Reflecting Children's Lives*. If the story was written for the first edition, we have asked the author to write a postscript reflecting on her story a decade later. For inspiration and a vision of where you might travel on your teaching journey, consider reading and discussing these stories with your coworkers or classmates.

What You'll Discover

This handbook was developed to help you develop yourself as an early childhood professional. It is primarily focused on planning for three- to five-year-old children, but throughout it includes ideas relevant to even younger children. To give infants and toddlers the additional attention they deserve, a specific chapter is focused on this age group. You may be using this book as a text for a class you are taking. Or you may discover it as a resource for curriculum planning for yourself or others you are mentoring. Teachers, education coordinators, administrators, and college instructors will find ideas and strategies here to create places for childhood that include intellectually engaging activities and opportunities to explore learning domain content in meaningful ways.

This handbook is designed to help you chart your own thinking as you consider new possibilities for your curriculum planning. Throughout the book you'll note this icon [icon] where materials are available on the web. These web enhancements include a beginning reflection exercise, an activity to practice the ideas, and questions to guide your reflections on the teachers' stories at the end of each chapter. We've included e-mail addresses so you can actually communicate with these teachers. Copies of charts, forms, and assessment tools are also available on the Redleaf Press website. Go to www.redleafpress.org. Type "Reflecting Children's Lives" in the search box and follow the link to the book. Links for the web-based materials are provided there.

Chapter 1 begins with self-assessment activities. Whenever you set about learning something new, you should begin with what you already know and feel. Use the checklists, comparative charts, and questions to make note of your present knowledge and experiences before you move through the chapters that follow. Your notes will give you a reference for considering what you want to learn from the book.

The foundation of curriculum planning and child guidance is the learning environment you create. Chapter 2 includes quick checklists for assessing your current learning environment for key elements of childhood: cultivating dreams and imagination, reflecting real lives, and providing for physical power and adventure. There are suggestions for designing your space, establishing a schedule, and developing classroom routines. There are also lists of open-ended materials that help you create a "loose parts" curriculum. You'll find six basic guidelines for transforming your teaching. This chapter ends with an inspiring story of how one program used these ideas to create an outdoor play space.

In this second edition of *Reflecting Children's Lives,* we've included a new chapter on guiding children as they play and learn. Chapter 3 outlines the limitations of relying on behavior management techniques and offers specific suggestions for goals you might have in guiding children to become self-regulating. Considerations for how you use your adult power are offered, along with an examination of how to see a child's intentions in his or her behavior. The story at the end of this chapter is from a mentor-teacher who helps teachers see the importance of giving children opportunities to think, problem solve, and develop self-control.

Chapter 4 offers a view of developmentally appropriate practice as fundamentally attending to who the children are and what is meaningful to them. To do so, you must sharpen your observation and documentation skills. You'll find practice activities to help you, here in the book and also on the web. This all comes to life in a story of how a student intern in a Head Start program started using her observations to learn things from the children that she thought she already knew. She goes on to carefully study her observations with her coworkers to support a child's dream to build a castle on their playground.

In chapter 5, you'll be asked to reconsider your approach to theme planning. We offer activities to remind you of the stages of play as defined by Piaget, followed by suggestions of materials that will enhance your ability to provide for the themes of meaningful work, physical development, creative expression, transformation activities, and learning useful skills. You'll find children's projects to analyze and teacher responses to consider. This chapter closes with two stories from masterful teachers whose deep respect for children leads each of them to an extensive curriculum project based on their passion for fairness and countering the limitations of stereotypes.

Given today's educational climate, we've added a new chapter 6 for this edition. It focuses on teaching academics in a meaningful way within the context of your everyday living and learning with children. We offer examples with regard to expanding children's learning in language, literacy, math, science, and technology, stressing the importance of continually helping children to learn how to learn. This chapter closes with another lively example of a teacher carefully studying her documentation to enhance her understandings and planning by, in this case, researching how children learn to write.

Curriculum for infants and toddlers must be centered around building relationships, a foundational element that opens chapter 7. Building relationships involves knowing the developmental themes of this time of life, reading cues and responding as an improvisational artist. This expanded chapter provides ideas about how to use caregiving routines as a source of curriculum, and it offers lists of interesting, low-cost materials to engage the lively minds of the youngest children. In her story at the end of this chapter, a teacher describes working with toddlers as akin to "riding the waves."

Chapter 8 will help you organize and communicate your approach to child-centered curriculum planning. You'll find several alternative approaches to filling out tiny boxes on a weekly schedule to use in your curriculum planning. We've included examples that other educators have used. Here we've compiled all the desired learning outcomes for children suggested in each of the other chapters and put them in a form you can use for assessment. You'll find several activities (which you can take up independently) to help you strengthen your ability to communicate the value of what you are doing with coworkers or with classmates. The story at the end of this chapter is an example of a teacher who has learned to narrate her self-discovery as she works with children.

For further consideration of your professional journey, chapter 9 includes different ways to think about the roles you play with children, dispositions to cultivate in yourself, and ways to enhance your own sense of wonder and aesthetics. You'll find questions to reflect on your teacher roles and dispositions, and ways you can continue to cultivate your own joy of learning. Finally, you'll hear a teacher's story of perseverance with his career, even when some of his workplaces aren't supporting his heart, intuition, and growing knowledge of child-centered planning. He shares turning points on his professional journey, including a college class designed for discovery and a Head Start administrator who encouraged him to be innovative and take risks.

Because of the ever-expanding resources now available on the Internet, we've chosen not to include a list of recommended resources at the end of this book. You can keep current with our resources as authors by visiting www.redleafpress.org, where we will be continually adding new web enhancements to our books. To contact us and see where our work is taking us, visit www.ecetrainers.com.

A Work in Progress

Think of *Reflecting Children's Lives* as your work in progress. Use the space provided on many pages to take notes and record a question, a memory of a related experience or idea, or something you need help with. Use this book at your own pace, alone or with colleagues. Take time to complete the suggested activities in the text and with our web enhancements, and make note of things you already know as well as things you still don't understand. Use it as a workbook that you return to for inspiration and ideas. See it as a record of the development of your own thinking and practice.

You may recognize some ideas on these pages from other books that we or our colleagues have written. They appear here as ideas worth repeating and as strategies for planning curriculum for the children in your program and for setting goals for your professional growth. Draw on this book when you need to rethink what you're doing or when you're planning to lead workshops and classes. Use it to help you mentor new teachers, volunteers, substitutes, or parents in your classroom. Our hope is that *Reflecting Children's Lives* will not only help you plan effectively for your early childhood setting, but will enhance your ability to stand for children. Use every opportunity you can to speak up for the childhood experiences and lively minds our youngest citizens deserve to have us invest in.

Begin with Yourself

➤ Beginning Reflections

Could One of These Teachers Be You?

Verna is a positive, upbeat teacher. She loves children and conscientiously pursues her curriculum goals, following the latest information available to preschool teachers. She continually tries out new activities from curriculum books. Verna has her ups and downs but says her classroom runs well. Increasingly, she's struggling to meet all the new early learning guidelines, and she's unsettled, with nagging doubts about her teaching. Many of the activities she plans don't seem very meaningful to the children; they just rush through them, eager to move on to the next thing. A small voice inside her triggers closer examination and questions about what's going on.

Isabel has been a family child care provider for two years. She offers a relaxed home environment with a variety of toys for the children to play with. She believes in letting kids do what they want. During the last few months, however, Isabel has been taking classes that suggest she needs to be offering more learning activities for the children in her care. She's saving money to buy some new toys and thinks she'll get some work sheets and craft books to try out these new ideas, but she's not sure how they will work.

Michael teaches in a government-funded preschool program. Much of his time is spent completing paperwork—forms, reports, lesson plans, and assessments. He diligently tries to make his classroom reflect the standards and regulations that are requirements of his job. His time with children is tightly scheduled, and he has developed effective classroom management techniques with a variety of entertaining routines. Recently he has begun to feel the joy he used to have working with kids is being overshadowed by all these required tasks. When he's honest with himself, he admits he isn't building real relationships with the children. He doesn't really understand how all of the paperwork connects with his work with children. He's just going through all of the motions.

Welcome to the Journey

Opening this handbook reveals a journey many providers and teachers are on—searching for a curriculum that is more alive and meaningful for the children and themselves while keeping up with all the current changes in the field. As you join in this search, you have probably begun to question by looking thoughtfully and with new eyes at what is happening in your classroom. Perhaps you are looking for support for how to negotiate all of these challenges. Let's see what you will discover. Read through the list below and check what's true for you.

Have you asked yourself why you plan your curriculum the way you do?

- ☐ Do you follow the same daily routines and curriculum plans because it's the way you've always done it?

- ☐ Do you obediently follow rules and regulations, not knowing or questioning the reasons why they exist?

- ☐ Have you noticed that the children are restless and bored and that you are too?

- ☐ Does your program reflect what you and the children really care about?

Is your work life stressful and fast-paced—your time filled with a continuous cycle of activity preparation and cleanup; parent notes, curriculum plans, reports, and newsletters to write; and e-mails, notices, new regulations, and articles to read?

☐ Do you have few opportunities to slow down and spend quality time with children?

☐ Are you exhausted at the end of each day, more because of what didn't happen with the kids than because of what did?

Are you concerned because your program has been invaded by commercialism and the media's idea of childhood?

☐ Do children's toys, lunch boxes, and clothes reflect the latest super-hero products from TV and movies?

☐ Do you find the children following the scripts of these violent and stereotyped characters with play that is repetitive and lacking in creativity?

☐ Do most of your interactions with children involve preventing fights and soothing hurt feelings?

☐ Have you noticed that many toys are designed and packaged with predetermined themes and offer limited opportunity for investigation, invention, or using one's own ideas or imagination?

☐ Are you concerned that when you provide open-ended, challenging activities and toys the children won't know how to begin without your help and some may be reluctant to even try?

Do you ever feel it's time to reexamine the icons of preschool culture— circle time, calendar time, cleanup time, paper plate and paper bag art projects, holiday themes, or the value of learning the ABC song?

☐ Do your holiday projects create additional stress and exhaustion for you and the children and convey an underlying message of commercialism?

☐ Have any children in your program been overlooked because you assumed all families celebrate and value traditional Christian or European American–based holidays?

☐ Have you discovered that getting children ready for kindergarten often really means teaching to the standards rather than engaging children's minds?

☐ When you reflect on children's play, do you really understand how to support the learning quest they are on?

The Three Rs Aren't Enough

Findings in brain development and early childhood learning theory demonstrate that children thrive and learn within the context of loving relationships. Children grow when curriculum activities are meaningful and geared to their interests and developmental and cultural needs. They reach new understandings as a result of attentive adults who scaffold their learning. They develop positive self-esteem, social skills, and confidence when their family life and culture are part of the life of the classroom.

At the heart of children's learning is active play in an engaging environment—uninterrupted time to curiously explore, to become physically competent, and to be intellectually engaged. Adults enhance children's learning with support to extend these experiences and deepen their understandings.

Yet, in early education today, we see an ever-increasing "push-down" curriculum with an emphasis on "academic readiness." Kindergarten feels too much like first grade, and thus, preschool expectations resemble the view of kindergarten that was held a couple decades ago. This shift reflects the notion that children have to be given formal lessons at an earlier and earlier age in order to be successful. There is also the more subtle implication that children can't be trusted to learn through their play, that play is wasting valuable time that could be devoted to preparing for school. This "get them ready" emphasis leads to a preschool curriculum that is too abstract for young children's concrete thinking and often includes meaningless memorization and parroting. To be sure, some children need to be guided to learn how to benefit from playing. They have spent more time in front of a television or computer screen than outside and aren't always sure how to direct themselves or join with peers in creating dramas and games. A combination of stressed, busy lives, media hype, and fears for their child's safety and school success has led parents to restructure their children's lives and eliminate open-ended play. Today's children typically need guidance in how to get into play, pursue an interest, or make new friends. Teachers can provide support to help children become self-initiated players, investigators, and inventors. Providing an engaging environment for active, rich play and offering coaching on needed skills can reestablish play as the foundation for children's learning.

In contrast to this vision of learning through play, a simplified version of the "Three Rs" doesn't capture children's imaginations or engage their minds. It leads to behavior problems and teacher burnout. There are, however, more significant and satisfying "Rs" for children and teachers to learn. Here is a list of a few of our favorites:

More Rs to Learn

Remember to slow down. Take time to really notice and delight in children and the magic of their development.

Reawaken yourself and the children to a sense of wonder, curiosity, a passion for discovery, and new learning.

Reevaluate your goals and focus your curriculum on relationships with people, nature, and the learning process.

Recognize that childhood is a time for intense intellectual pursuits as well as social and emotional learning. Build curriculum on children's interests and on the questions and skills they are pursuing.

Revisit the idea of academic lessons. Rather than work sheets, offer children hands-on opportunities to gain understanding of math, science, reading, writing, and experimentation.

Respond to children's need for time. Provide opportunities and coaching that allow children to investigate and practice a skill over and over again at their own speed. Extended, engaged activity helps children deepen their understandings and build confidence. Having time to explore and express oneself nourishes a love for learning.

Refocus your celebrations on meaningful events and accomplishments that occur as a part of the daily life of your classroom. Create rituals and representations to help everyone pay attention to the miracles of life, the joys of discovery, and the community they can create together.

Reinforce collaboration rather than competition. Provide activities, experiences, and materials that encourage working together rather than working in isolation.

Reconnect with your community. Plan the majority of activities in your curriculum around real people, real issues, and real work being done in your community.

Represent the interests, activities, and thinking process that is the heart of your program. Take time to observe, record, and create displays with photos, stories, and celebrations honoring the events in your daily lives together.

Renew yourself often! Give yourself regular time for self-reflection and self-care. Indulge in collaborative thinking and working with friends and colleagues. You can't care for others if you haven't taken care of yourself.

Revive your activism on behalf of children and yourself. Children need caring adults to champion the importance of childhood and the value of play, joyful discovery, and feeling alive in our bodies. Those in the early childhood profession need advocates for recognition, respect, and adequate compensation for the valuable work they do.

Adding these "Rs" into your work does not mean adding more stress to your already busy life. Rather, it implies slowing down and building from what's already available within and around you, in the children, in families, and in the community. It only requires that you observe carefully, think critically, and cultivate your own passion for childhood.

The focus of a child-centered curriculum is on the children—their curiosities and desires to learn. As you read through the following chart, think about what these concepts would mean to the children in your class. Which approach would excite them? Which would help them to participate and open up to you?

Traditional Approaches

Teachers believe the primary purpose of preschool is to give children a head start on academic lessons and to become accustomed to school routines and expectations.

Teacher planning is focused only on group times and art projects, neglecting regular changes to the environment to continually extend curiosity and possibilities.

Curriculum activities are focused on academic lessons, work sheets, arts and crafts products, and topical themes presented to children during group time. These activities often result in look-alike products that children can take home to demonstrate what they are learning in preschool.

Teachers ignore most nondisruptive, child-initiated play. Instead, they do housekeeping and record-keeping tasks during "free choice time." Free play is offered for short periods of time and is seen as a break from the curriculum.

Child-Centered Approaches

Teachers put play at the heart of the curriculum. They support play with ample time, materials, and thoughtful coaching.

Teachers plan the environment as the basis for the curriculum, which is child-centered and reflects the children's interests and lives. Materials are in good condition, are interesting, and are organized with attention to aesthetics.

Teachers understand that children are active, sensory learners who need many opportunities for self-chosen exploration, social interaction, and problem solving. They are more interested in the learning process than in planning products to teach something or to show off the curriculum.

Teachers observe the play of individuals and groups, noting aspects of their physical, cognitive, social, and emotional development. Teachers make mental or written notes regarding the children's questions, skills, and frustrations.

Traditional Approaches	Child-Centered Approaches
Teacher-directed curriculum themes overshadow or hide children's interests. Look-alike products are displayed on the bulletin boards, with no sign of children's imagination or engagement.	Teachers use children's "themes" as the basis for curriculum planning. Planning involves introducing materials and interactions that stimulate the emergence of the children's ideas and understandings.
Teachers police the room, keeping children on task, regulating the use of materials, and disciplining children who haven't developed social skills.	As the children engage with materials provided, teachers observe and become involved with children's investigations, offer questions and guidance, and plan enrichment activities to add to the environment.
Teachers base their curriculum plans around traditional school topics, popular cultural holidays, and prepackaged seasonal curriculum theme books.	Teachers share their own passions, interests, and questions, which may serve as another source of children's interests and curriculum.
Curriculum plans are pulled from files or curriculum books and are repeated on an annual basis as "topics to be covered."	Written curriculum plans document the children's involvement with materials, questions, and discoveries, rather than documenting activities teachers will direct.
Teachers focus their planning for individual children on academic deficiencies and the need for repetitive practice of the school readiness skills the children have yet to acquire.	For typically developing children, individual planning addresses children's frustrations by focusing on their strengths. Teachers seek the child's point of view in pursuing any readiness agenda.

Read through the chart again. This time, think about your own approach to curriculum and curriculum planning. What activities, room decorations, and role plays have you planned that utilize the traditional approach? What have you tried (or would like to try) that would foster and encourage the child-centered approach?

Analyzing Curriculum Plans

Now that you know there is more to the Three Rs and have thought about curriculum from a child's point of view, read through two curricula for the month of October. Melissa's and Sharon's plans reflect two very different ways of thinking about curriculum activities for young children. As you read through each plan, analyze the teacher's approach. Keep the following questions in mind to help you focus your analysis:

- What teacher goals do these curriculum plans suggest?

- How does the teacher think the children learn?

- What are the sensory aspects of each curriculum?

- What values—religious, commercial, diversity—are promoted by each plan?

- How does the curriculum plan draw on the children's daily lives and experiences?

- How does the teacher perceive her role in the learning process?

Melissa's Traditional October Curriculum

Themes

- scary things (witches, bats, black cats, spiders)

- trick-or-treat

- costumes

Room Environment

- commercial cutouts: jack-o'-lanterns, witches, skeletons
- spider webs hanging on wall
- children's finished Halloween art projects

Art Projects

- paper-plate pumpkins: paint plates orange and paste on black face shapes
- construction paper spiders: attach precut legs to body and hang
- scary night: crayon drawings of "spooky" pictures sponged with black
- ghost print: use white tempera on black construction paper
- stand-up pumpkins: glue colored pumpkin activity sheets on cardboard
- trick-or-treat bags: Halloween shapes cut out by the teacher, glued on paper bags
- pumpkin accordion people: accordion-fold strips glued on body parts of pumpkin-head people
- egg carton witch: egg carton sections decorated as witches with collage materials and precut face pieces to glue on

Games and Movement Activities

- The Old Witch and the Cat: one child is the witch, the others sit in a circle and are cats; the witch hobbles around the circle with a blindfold; one of the cats meows; the witch tries to guess who that child is
- Spiders and Flies: tag game with some children as flies, some as spiders
- Ghost, Ghost, Witch: a variation of Duck, Duck, Goose
- Jack-O'-Lantern Bean Bag Throw: throw bean bags into plastic jack-o'-lanterns

Poems and Songs

- "Halloween Time"
- "Five Little Ghosts"
- "Five Little Jack-o'-Lanterns"
- "How Does a Goblin Go?"
- "Cackle, Cackle, Ugly Witch"

Books

- *Ghost's Hour, Spook's Hour* by Eve Bunting
- *The Little Witch's Halloween Book* by Linda Glovach
- *The Night before Halloween* by Natasha Wing
- *Scary, Scary Halloween* by Eve Bunting
- *The Tooth Witch* by Nurit Karlin

Special Activities

- carving a pumpkin: children help teacher decide what kind of jack-o'-lantern face to have on a pumpkin and watch while it is carved
- a Halloween party: children wear costumes from home (Indian, Batman, Buzz Lightyear, Ironman, Barbie, princess, bride, pirate, hobo, Spiderman, the Incredibles, etc.); trick-or-treat within program classrooms; jack-o'-lantern cupcakes, witch's brew, and Halloween candy as party treats
- cooking projects: spooky gelatin spiders; monster toast; witch's brew; jack-o'-lantern fruit cup

A Closer Look

Melissa's October curriculum is probably familiar to most of us, as it centers on the traditional practice of using commercialized, European American holidays as the focus for planning.

In this approach, children are consumers of activities and images rather than inventors. Melissa offers preplanned, premade, and simplistic projects. She overlooks the opportunity to have the children explore their own understandings and underlying rationale for the project. The children may think a lot of this is fun, but there is no real, honest connection to their lives beyond the commercial holiday hype. There is even less sensory exploration or active participation.

Most teachers argue that children love Halloween. Upon closer examination, however, we can see that children really don't love commercialized cuteness or stereotypical costumes or being frightened. What they do love is the magic and drama that come with make-believe play and dress up. They love the power of acting out a role and the surprise of transforming themselves and the world around them.

With these ideas in mind, analyze another October curriculum using the same questions provided at the beginning of this section.

Sharon's Child-Centered October Curriculum

Themes

- autumn harvest, end of the growing season (death)

- surprise, transforming materials

- masks, dress up, role play

Room Environment

- objects from outdoors: dead vines and leaves, pinecones, gourds, pumpkins, nuts, bones

- rotting and molding pumpkin: magnifying glass; small container for composting to watch decaying process

- photographs of children on field trips to pumpkin farm and apple orchard

- children's dictation: stories of their experiences on the field trips and in the classroom

- display table honoring people and pets who have died: photographs from home, dictated stories

Sensory and Cooking Activities

- pumpkin cutting: children each help cut their own pumpkin; explore the seeds, texture, smell, taste

- roasting and tasting pumpkin seeds

- baking pumpkin pie and custard

- washing, coring, and peeling apples

- making applesauce

- tasting and comparing different kinds of apples

- harvesting and drying: apples, herbs, and flowers

- making and drinking: mint, chamomile, and ginger teas

- grinding and tasting: spices such as cinnamon, nutmeg, and cloves
- making and eating: soups such as pumpkin, squash, potato, and vegetable
- making and mixing: magic brews of food color and water, oil and water, cornstarch and water, baking soda and vinegar
- enhancing the sensory table: pinecones, leaves, cinnamon sticks, dried flowers, mint, and nuts
- cracking and eating: nuts
- smelling and kneading: black playdough scented with spices of cloves, cinnamon, vanilla, almond, peppermint extracts; some with glitter

Classification and Sorting

- apples
- squashes
- seeds and nuts
- leaves
- pinecones
- herbs and flowers

Dramatic Play and Dress-Up

- prop boxes: a variety of fabrics, scarves, hats, jewelry, shoes, capes, wands, and pouches; children create their own costumes and dramatic play roles
- face painting: nontoxic face paints, with mirrors, camera; related books about fiestas, celebrations
- warm clothes: mittens, hats, afghans, boots in dress-up area

Art Activities

- collage materials
- papier-mâché to make masks
- glitter, feathers, fabric, paper scraps

- full range of paint colors
- drawing and cutting implements
- a variety of ways to attach things together (including glue, stapler, tape, hole punches, brads, yarn, and rings)

Music and Movement

- a variety of musical styles (classical, blues, nature sounds)
- harvest and fall songs
- move like animals, the weather, leaves, trees
- dance with scarves and feathers

Books

- *The Barn Dance* by Bill Martin Jr., and John Archambault
- *Frederick* by Leo Lionni
- *From Seed to Pumpkin* by Wendy Pfeffer
- *In a Nutshell* by Joseph Anthony
- *Lifetimes* by Bryan Mellonie
- *The Little Old Lady Who Was Not Afraid of Anything* by Linda Williams
- *The Moon Was at a Fiesta* by Matthew Gollub
- *Pablo Remembers the Fiesta of the Day of the Dead* by George Ancona
- *The Pumpkin Blanket* by Deborah Turney Zagwyn
- *Rain Makes Applesauce* by Julian Scheer
- *The Tenth Good Thing about Barney* by Judith Viorst
- various science and nature books
- children's dictated stories made into books

Special Activities and Field Trips

- trips to pumpkin patch and apple orchard to get food for cooking
- discussion with families about visits to the cemetery

A Closer Look

As autumn arrives, Sharon knows children's senses are aroused in response to the changes they notice. Her October curriculum reflects the concrete and sensory aspects of children's daily experiences. She plans ways for them to explore and learn more about what they can see, hear, and smell all around them.

Sharon provides materials and activities that fully engage children's bodies and senses. She offers opportunities for exploration at a more complex level, with observation of the more important themes of trying on new roles, being powerful, life and death, and transformation of materials, nature, and people. Sharon has planned fully for process and investigation, rather than products and clichés. The children are creators of this curriculum.

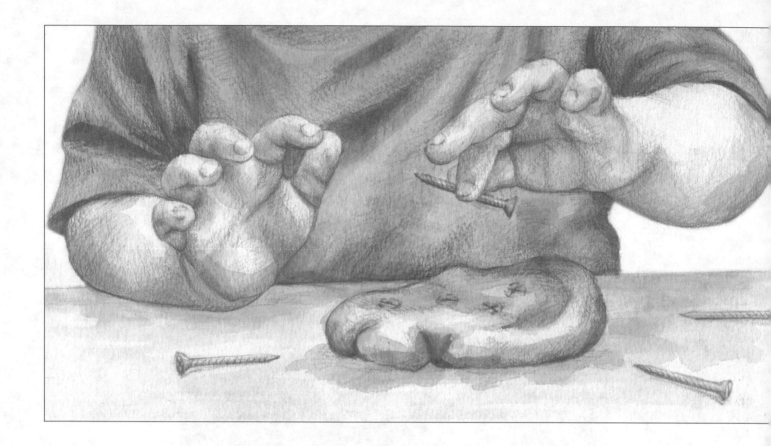

An Inspirational Story

To be a good teacher means you are always a learner. In the following story, Kelly Matthews, a family child care provider, describes how a child took her curriculum plan one step further than she had expected. She recognized this and the deeper complexity of what the child was recognizing.

The Impression Ben Made

Kelly Matthews, Family Child Care Provider

There are times when I have thought I was in control of the educational process I provided in my classroom. On those days, things went along as planned, and I would say to myself, "This is a good day. This is how it was supposed to be." I planned these activities, then kids would watch a bit, try it out themselves, and "get it," taking away from the process what I had entered in my mental lesson plan for the day. My job as a teacher was complete. After all, that was what I was being paid to do—teach the kids what to do.

After awhile, this process began to feel flat. Something was missing, even though my teaching was often complimented. While I heard from outside sources I was doing a good job, I felt conflicted. I could tell something wasn't right, even though kids were working with materials, listening to directions, and getting along with each other. I couldn't ignore the voice inside saying *more is possible*—something not so predictable; something that was more than making sure kids followed what was in each day's little boxes.

Listening to that voice was the beginning of a new way. Even though I ended up changing settings, I was able to keep that voice alive, and in fact, it became a guiding voice. I thought back over my assumptions about what a teacher's job was. Previously, I had thought that it was about teaching kids *what to do,* but I realized this was a false idea. My job was to help them *think,* make that thinking explicit, and help them to act on that thinking. This was a completely different way to approach my interactions with my students. Instead of planning activities that would (superficially) expose them to a number of topics over the week, month, or year, I began spending more time with open-ended objects that let us—both the children and me—explore, bump up against problems, and then figure out how to solve those problems. I also stepped back from acting as expert (bringing something to show them, as well as showing them how to interact with it or do it before letting them practice).

I had another important realization. Even though I knew a lot about certain things (dinosaurs, playdough, and the other staples of many early education programs), I didn't know what my students *knew;* I only knew what they could repeat back. More importantly, I didn't know how they came to the "knowing" of ideas. How were they constructing their personal knowledge?

What would they do with it? What would it take for them to change a held idea? What connections would they make between experiences?

I embraced curiosity. It was a way to be true to this dynamic process, and I became a learner alongside my students. One day I set out sets of dough and screws. As Ben was working with his dough and screws, I called attention to the method I used to make a full-length impression. He made one himself, *but then he took it one step further by building on my idea with one of his own.* He started making impressions with just the head of the screws. He paid careful attention to the marks he made. Some were Phillips head screws, while others were flathead screws. Ben picked up another screw, examined the head, and exclaimed, "This one's different!" *even before making an impression in the dough.* Here was a child making *connections.*

As a teacher-learner in that moment, I realized that in giving Ben a method of making imprints, he took up that idea but went even further than what I had expected. If I would have done a lesson limited to "making an impression," I would have missed this moment in which Ben showed his inquisitiveness, flexible thinking, and ability to bring knowledge to a new context and apply it. I have come to understand it's not only what Ben learns, but what he teaches me about *how* he learns that is invaluable.

I sometimes forget what a complicated, collaborative process education is. Luckily I have children like Ben who remind me.

Share Your Reflections with Kelly

Write a letter to Kelly at KMatthewsReflect@gmail.com with your reflections on how she was learning to rethink her approach to curriculum. Consider including your thoughts about the following:

- What did Kelly think she was "missing" in her approach to curriculum planning?

- How did she use the environment and materials to learn about the children's perspectives?

- What new insights did she have about her role as a teacher?

▶ *Practice What You've Learned*

Notes about Your Current Approach to Curriculum Planning

Use this space to reflect on your approach to curriculum planning. Use these questions to get started.

When you begin planning curriculum, what is your process, your starting place, your focus?

_____

_____

_____

_____

When you look over previous curriculum plans you've developed, what do they offer that includes or involves complexity and experiences that are meaningful for the children?

_____

_____

_____

_____

How could you improve your current curriculum approach using the information from this chapter?

_____

_____

_____

_____

Revitalizing the Environment

2

► Beginning Reflections

Think about your home. What rooms do you feel most comfortable in? What elements and objects reflect who you are, what you care about, your history and interests? What are you drawn to because of its beauty? What gives you the most pleasure to look at, touch, listen to? What excites your mind, what makes you curious and eager to learn more?

Environments beyond the Basics

Our environments have a great influence on how we feel and behave and what we pay attention to. This is especially true for children in early childhood programs. If children spend their waking hours in disorganized, unattractive places, it will influence how they behave, what they are learning, and who they become.

The environment is the foundation of any early childhood curriculum. Most books on early childhood environments describe the basics of organizing a preschool classroom—defined activity areas and age-appropriate materials that are visible and accessible. Although these basics are important for a child-centered curriculum, quality early childhood programs must go beyond the basics. The environment should be intriguing and aesthetically pleasing. It should be inviting and cultivate children's curiosity, wonder, and imagination. We offer you some starting points here and recommend that you read our detailed book on environments, *Designs for Living and Learning* (2003).

Take the Child's Point of View

Take a minute to examine your classroom environment. Does it go beyond clean and orderly to encourage curiosity and joyful exploration? Get down on your knees and look at the entire space from a child's point of view. Are there things that spark your curiosity and make you want to touch and investigate? Are those things within your reach? If your friends came here to play with you, would there be enough room? Can you find things to use as props in your play? Do you see things that make you feel at home?

While you're down on your knees in your classroom looking at things from a child's perspective, read through the following checklist. Mark the things that are true about your environment.

"On-Your-Knees" Checklist

☐ Materials are visible, accessible, aesthetically organized, and attractive to children.

☐ Diverse textures, shapes, and elements of the natural world are present to invite exploration and discovery.

☐ The space is flexible, allowing for expansion when many children are working in the same area. There are minimal restrictions to moving in and out of areas.

☐ In addition to specialized toys such as pretend food, wooden blocks, and Lego building blocks, there is an ample supply of "loose parts"—open-ended materials such as large pieces of fabric, corks, tubes, and plastic rings.

☐ Children's lives and interests are represented throughout the room; there are work samples, photos, sketches, homemade books, and objects with stories.

☐ Visual images represent a range of roles and cultural expressions that can help children learn about similarities and differences.

Now review the list. How many points have check marks by them? Not too many? Most of them? Are you surprised at the results? The following sections provide strategies that can help you create an environment where both you and the children will love to spend time.

Cultivate Dreams and Imagination

Begin enriching environments for children (and yourself) by paying attention to aesthetics and creating a sense of wonder and curiosity. Consider the typical classroom—bright primary colors, cute cartoon drawings and commercial characters on the displays and toys, and materials made of plastic and other synthetics.

This environment may be utilitarian and easy to stock, but what does it say about our values, what we believe about children and the teaching and learning process? A typical preschool environment often overstimulates children, when it should instead provoke their curiosity or imagination. The room feels more commercial than inviting, cozy, or filled with natural wonders to explore.

As you look around your room and think about making it more inviting and aesthetically pleasing, consider three important elements: storage, lighting, and aesthetics.

Ideas for Storage and Arrangement of Materials

Thoughtful storage and display of materials will convey a natural sense of order as well as beauty. Remember the principle "less is more," and rotate materials in and out of storage, depending on the learning goals you are emphasizing and the children's interests during a particular period. Accessible storage and an orderly presentation of materials invites children's focus and curiosity and encourages children to appreciate and use materials more intentionally.

- Children are drawn more easily to materials if they are offered in containers made of natural materials and neutral colors with wide openings, and placed so children can see what is inside them.

- Easy-to-find storage and display ideas include straw baskets; wooden bowls; trays; clear plastic tubs, boxes, and jars; hat boxes; and containers with interesting textures and aesthetic qualities.

- Placing mirrors (all sizes and shapes) with materials on top of them in unexpected places around the room highlights the materials so children discover new possibilities for exploration.

Ideas for Lighting

Pay close attention to the lighting in your environment. Thoughtful use of light and shadows can awaken children to new perspectives, enchantment, and excitement about learning.

- Whenever possible, fill your classroom with natural light.
- Hang things in windows that blow in the breeze, create rainbows, or cast shadows in the room.
- Use safety lamps, dimmer switches, and other sources of indirect lighting throughout the environment. In some places, use colored lightbulbs or theater gel to highlight areas or create special moods.
- Light candles (in enclosed containers and out of children's reach) for meals and naptime to signal special times and rituals of the day. You may want to consider battery-powered candles to avoid asthma triggers and other toxins that some candles release into the air.
- Place mirrors on walls, shelves, and counters to reflect light and images and create a spacious feeling.

Ideas for Softness and Pleasure

Fill your early childhood environment with things that will create interest, warmth, and pleasure for the senses. Avoid rugs and fabrics with "busy patterns"; coordinate colors so children are not bombarded or overstimulated. Be intentional about your choices, ensuring the atmosphere is calm and supports the children's focus. Be on the lookout for items like these at garage sales, flea markets, and secondhand stores:

- straw mats

- throw rugs

- pillows, cushions, and bean bag chairs

- fabric of diverse textures, colors, thickness, and patterns from various cultures

- art prints and postcards

- nature photography and posters

- sculpture, pottery, natural baskets, and other forms of art

- lap quilts and soft blankets

Use Elements of Nature

In our safety- and liability-conscious world, children are kept indoors or behind fences with materials and equipment made from plastic, concrete, and cold, hard metal. They have fewer and fewer opportunities to experience the pleasures of the natural world and the sensory delights of playing with soft, natural materials. Many studies show that ongoing exposure to nature is vital for the health and well-being of humans.

You can provide more experiences with nature for children, indoors and outdoors, in simple, inexpensive ways. Set up sensory tables filled with sand and water; create areas with natural materials for investigation; bring in plants, pets, and gardens to care for.

Ideas from the Natural World

- Place large boulders or tree stumps around the room and use them for seating or as small workspaces, for indoor climbing or an obstacle course, or as dividers to define areas of the room.

- Add twigs, rocks, shells, feathers, leaves, driftwood, marble, and other natural materials to activity centers. In the block area, they

become part of the building and architecture. In the dramatic play area, they become food for people and animals. On tables, they are items for counting and classifying. In the art area, they become a part of children's sensory exploration, collage, and representations.

- Include a variety of plants, trees, and flowers throughout the room. Use hanging baskets to lower ceilings and add a cozy feeling. Create a reading area where children can sit under the branch of a tree. Add plants and flowers to shelves and tables where children eat. Construct a fishpond with lily pads, indoors or outdoors. (You can find reasonably priced kits in nurseries and home stores.)

- Add a small bubbling fountain or waterfall to your classroom. (Again, look for kits in nurseries and home stores.)

Keep Space and Classroom Routines Flexible

A child-centered curriculum is about creating spaces that preserve childhood and provoke a love of learning. It involves slowing down and paying attention to all of the possibilities for beauty, curiosity, engaged investigation, delight, and a sense of community in your classroom.

Rich curriculum is possible with each routine, including meals, cleanup, self-care, and moving from place to place; with each interaction involving inquiry, shared excitement, and problem solving; with time on the child's side, which means long periods of time to play, focusing on interests and practice skills and friendships.

The environment sets the stage by creating an atmosphere and opportunity for engagement. Rather than structuring the classroom with rigid rules and routines, the space, the rules, and the adults must be flexible. To work as a guardian of childhood and promoter of active learning, you must be an improvisational artist—responding to needs, rearranging space, and creating new ways for discovery and relationships.

Classroom rules, routines, and arrangement of the environment create the ebb and flow of childhood. Too often our days with children are focused on getting them ready—to eat, to go outside, to take a nap, to hear a story, to go to school. With this get-them-ready mind-set, we miss the moment of *now* in childhood and the chance to meet real needs and interests. Research suggests complex play doesn't typically emerge until children have been actively engaged for about thirty minutes. In practice, this research implies fewer transitions, allowing longer stretches of time for deeper involvement. In a child-centered framework, curriculum is everything that happens—the planned as well as the unplanned activities, routines, transitions, arrivals, and departures.

Elements of a Child-Centered Curriculum

Consider these elements as you plan and respond to children:

- close relationships with the children's families and continuous efforts to include families in your thinking and planning

- space and materials that invite sustained engagement for continuous self-initiated play

- flexible space arrangements and routines to respond to children's involvement in play

- minimal adult agendas interrupting children's play

- flexible requirements about cleaning up before moving on to another area to continue a thread of engaged play

- child-initiated play themes incorporated into cleanup and group time routines

- little distinction between transitions and play

- turn-taking negotiated by children with teachers coaching, rather than intervening with rigid time limits

- invented rituals to deal with difficult transitions and times when things don't feel good, as well as milestones and celebrations

Seven Basic Principles for Transforming Your Teaching

As you move toward a curriculum that better reflects children's lives, these seven steps will provide a more meaningful and rich experience for you and the children in your care. They will also create a strong foundation for school readiness.

Principle: Set the stage and allow time.

Plan the environment as your basic curriculum, organizing the space
and materials in accessible, attractive, and inviting ways that suggest
all sorts of choices and possibilities. Allow at least one-hour blocks of
time for children to engage in open-ended free choice activities uninterrupted by adult agendas or schedule demands.

Principle: Open the space.

Let go of rigid rules that require props to stay in certain areas. Let
children combine different areas. If dress-up clothes cannot go out
of the dress-up area, how can children become outfitted cooks at the
playdough table or suited firefighters in the block area? Markers and
pens may be needed for making signs in the block or dress-up areas,
along with books for reading to doll babies or consulting in the design
of building construction. Stock your room with an ample supply of
open-ended materials (loose parts) that beg to be transported and
transformed.

Principle: Avoid interrupting significant play.

Your goal is to enable children to become truly absorbed in activities of
their own choosing and making. As children move through the stages of
play, they are able to sustain complex, cooperative play and language for
longer and longer periods of time. Interrupting these interactions with
adult agendas and activities defeats the goal of extending children's
attention span, self-regulation, and independence.

Principle: Keep the cleanup options open.

A well-meaning teacher, concerned that children learn to responsibly care for the room, often asks a child to stop and put away abandoned toys when the child is still in the middle of playing out a script. A fire-fighter responding to a 911 call wants to play out the story, not stop for a few minutes to pick up some discarded dress-up clothes. Quietly tidy up an area yourself, or observe when the play episode has reached a natural conclusion before asking the children to clean up. Practice most of your cleanup requirements at cleanup time rather than during playtime.

Principle: Refer children to each other.

Young children need to see themselves as competent and resourceful. When you notice a child in need of assistance, point out another child who might be able to help. Model, support, and coach these interactions so that children develop the disposition and skills to use each other as resources. Treat conflict resolution in a similar manner. Provide routines, materials, and activities that require more than one person to make them work.

Principle: Consciously observe for opportunities to coach and extend.

Chose your responses carefully and intentionally. Offer your adult wisdom and knowledge when children could benefit from some coaching with skills, materials, or language to further their ideas and pursuits. Join with children in their learning process. Offer your appreciation of their ideas and relate your real life experiences to theirs.

Principle: Think twice before intervening.

Remember, not all moments need to be teacher-teachable moments. Children deserve and benefit from time to pursue their own ideas, work out conflicts with each other, and have a little privacy.

Loose Parts

Large corporations create most children's toys and materials, which often serve as commercials for TV programs, video games, and movies.

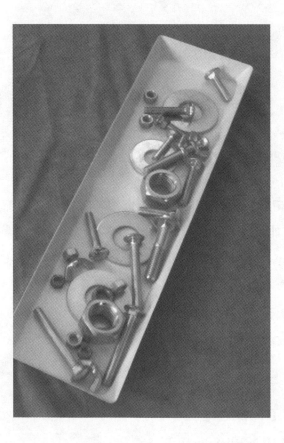

They come with a theme and a script, or a particular way to use them. How do these toys inspire children's investigation, imagination, or creativity? In most cases, they don't. Your task, then, is to provide open-ended materials that offer opportunities for transporting, transforming, and using one's experience and imagination.

Loose parts is a term coined by architect Simon Nicholson to refer to open-ended materials that provide opportunities for transporting, transforming, and using one's experience and imagination. Given the chance, children will use loose parts as invented props to support their play and investigation of the world. Children transport and transform loose parts in remarkable ways.

To add loose parts to your environment, look for interesting, open-ended materials. Yard sales and thrift stores, as well as your own forgotten boxes at home or in storage lockers, are great sources for these kinds of materials. Here are some of our favorite ideas for these curriculum enhancers.

Kitchen Curriculum

Every parent has a story of children preferring to play with pots, pans, and plastic tubs rather than a fancy new toy. Loose parts from the kitchen make great props for children's creative play. The most interesting gadgets are those with moveable parts or small compartments, such as sifters, tongs, jar openers, nutcrackers, egg holders, beaters, timers, ice cube trays, meat or cheese graters, garlic presses, melon ball scoopers, and vegetable steamers. Introduce these materials at circle time and again at choice time.

Rope, String, and Twine Curriculum

Assemble a box of rope, fabric belts, twine, string, yarn, shoelaces, and miscellaneous lengths of other ropelike materials. Provide them to children indoors or outdoors, as is, or with clothespins, pulleys, or clips. Watch the children come up with a multitude of uses, from exploring lengths and measuring to learning to tie to transporting objects. Coach children with safety guidelines when first introducing the use of ropes.

Farm Curriculum

Bales of straw are inexpensive loose parts to use outdoors (and indoors for courageous teachers!). When the bale is intact, children can use it for climbing, jumping, and elevating themselves. As the bale falls apart, loose straw becomes a soft place for jumping and hiding. It also can become a prop for dramatic play. Children can load, carry, build, and pretend to feed animals. (Check for allergies before using this curriculum.)

Cardboard Box Curriculum

Boxes are places to hide treasures, explore spatial relationships, and find privacy, alone or with a friend. Boxes spark all kinds of dramatic play and provide opportunities to transport objects from one place to another. Small boxes on tables offer an opportunity to practice sorting and classifying. Boxes are a free, never-ending source of rich curriculum for children. Get some today!

Fabric Curriculum

A collection of fabric in a variety of textures, shapes, and sizes is a great addition to a child-centered curriculum. Children use fabric for sensory exploration (wrapping up, seeing through), dramatic play (costumes, blankets), and construction (making tents and hiding places). They also explore spatial concepts by covering tables, blocks, themselves, and each other with fabric. Introduce fabrics in a variety of colors and diverse cultural designs as well as ones that are sheer, sequined, shiny, rough, thick, bumpy, lacy, and velvety.

Junk Shop Curriculum

Junk shops, thrift shops, and secondhand stores have many interesting gadgets that can become play props. (Check out your own junk storage areas too!) Sometimes you don't even know why the gadget was invented. The best ones come apart and fit together or open and close. Here are some ideas: doorknobs, switches, clamps, pipes, large nuts, bolts, hinges, pulleys, paint rollers, elastic cords, wrenches, hand tools, and old appliances to take apart. (Check for sharp edges, and cut cords and plugs off of electrical appliances. Also be mindful of toxins in PVC.)

Food Packaging and Odd Items Curriculum

Keep a shopping bag handy in your kitchen to collect clean food packaging, small boxes, paper towel rolls, and twists. Ask families to keep your classroom supplied as well. Seek out recycling and salvage businesses that have items for exploration and invention, such as all sizes and shapes of sponges and Styrofoam, paper bags and containers, rugs, wood, plastic and tile pieces, aluminum pans, wooden and plastic spools, old telephone wire, computer keyboards, and tape of all kinds, sizes, colors, and widths. (Many plastics contain chemicals that can be toxic. Children should be reminded not to chew on any plastic items or put items in their mouths.)

Honoring Childhood and Children's Lives

A child-centered curriculum reflects an understanding of the sensory, physical, and exploratory needs of children. In the preceding pages, you considered how to address these needs with your environment, materials, and activities.

Providing for children's social and emotional development is an equally important aspect of planning curriculum that reflects children's lives. True self-esteem is developed by focusing on children's identity, family life, and need for power and independence throughout the curriculum. Comfort with people different from oneself comes from meaningful opportunities to interact with others.

With these ideas in mind, take another look at your learning environment. Think about the following questions and use the space provided to jot down your reflections:

In what ways does the environment let children know that they belong?

_____

_____

_____

_____

How are children's lives and interests represented, honored, and celebrated?

_____

_____

_____

_____

What opportunities are available for children to see and explore who they are within the context of their family life, culture, and the larger community?

_____

_____

_____

_____

How do children learn empathy—not to fear, attack, or form biases against others different from themselves?

_____

_____

_____

_____

Where are the places for physical power and adventure that diminish a child's need to imitate media superheroes and violent characters?

_____

_____

_____

_____

Review your answers. If you discover that you want to make some improvements in this area, consider the following curriculum strategies.

Me and My Family

When children see their lives and interests reflected around them, they feel safe, known, and affirmed. Expand these representations of the children's lives with the school year:

- Create ongoing classroom displays and photo albums that include children's lives, past and present, at home and in preschool.

- Regularly incorporate food and positive mealtime experiences that are familiar to the children. This includes inviting parents to lead classroom cooking projects as part of the curriculum.

- Add books, pictures, and dramatic play props that reflect current family events and interests (e.g., birth of a new baby, moving, parent's job, and family celebrations).

- Make puzzles, matching games, and paper dolls for dramatic play using photos of the children, their families, and their homes and neighborhood. Enlarge the photos at a copy center, then mount and cut them out of heavy cardboard or foam core.

- Make "show and share" a daily part of your program. Rather than having one day for showing off commercial toys from home, add items with special meaning from home to your activity centers. Introduce these items with guidelines for use.

- Add a new activity area to your room: the Classroom and Community News Center. This can expand traditional "show and tell" routines with photos, stories, and children's work, as well as handmade books, family albums, and other objects from home. Add technology to this area with a laptop, whiteboard, or projectors. Include a digital camera, pens, paper, and ready-made blank books for children to participate in documenting the history of your time together in the classroom.

Learning about Others

Children are naturally curious about other people. With classification as a primary developmental theme, they are busy noticing similarities and differences. Provide opportunities for classification and comparison with images that show differences:

- Display pictures depicting the ways people carry different things—babies, water, and food. Add props such as baskets, backpacks, buckets, bamboo poles, and fabric slings for role-playing and dramatic play.

- Read books and post pictures reflecting the kinds of shelters where people live. Include both familiar places, such as houses, apartment buildings, and mobile homes, along with traditional types of dwellings in other cultures. Provide rocks, twigs, marble pieces, bales of straw, plaster of paris, leaves, and bamboo that can be used for construction activities.

- Bake different varieties of bread found across cultures, such as pita bread, fry bread, yeast bread, unleavened bread, hum bao, injera, bagels, naan, and croissants.

- Use photos of families in your program and pictures from children's books to explore the ways all kinds of families live together.

- Include different family compositions, cultures, celebrations, traditions, and living arrangements.

Countering Bias

Counter biased stereotypes by showing contemporary life and typical ways of living, rather than exotic activities or uncommon celebrations. Respond to fear of differences and the development of bias by incorporating some of the following activities into your curriculum:

- Create positive sensory experiences with various shades of brown and black (paint, clay, and playdough with extracts of vanilla, peppermint, licorice, and almond).

- Be aware of your language to ensure you don't perpetuate unintended stereotypes, such as only men are firefighters, doctors, or powerful people; only women are gentle and able to nurture; only people of color have culture; children always live with their parents; everyone celebrates Christian holidays; and all families have enough money for birthday parties.

- Respond positively to children who point out differences that they notice; help them feel that differences are normal, interesting, and welcome.

- Display photos of the children in your group embedded in a mural of children from all races and all economic conditions wearing all kinds of clothes.

Places for Physical Development Themes

A central developmental theme for preschoolers revolves around their bodies: how to live with their vulnerability and sense of powerlessness, and what to do with their ever-growing limbs and energy. Create places for physical power and adventure in your programs, inside and outside. Reclaim childhood from commercial interests.

Ripe with imagination, children naturally seek out representations of physical power and adventure to claim as their own. Too often we

trivialize children's needs for self-esteem and identity affirmation. We make comments such as, "What a big boy!" "Nice job!" and "That's so cute!" At the same time, we encourage children to suppress or negate their bodies and energy. We downplay—and thus hand over to TV, movies, video games, and commercial toys—children's need for adventure, risk taking, and boldness.

One way to provide for this extremely physical time of life is to develop obstacle courses. You can change them often to add ever-increasing challenges. Another way is to let children use real tools, do meaningful work, and take acceptable risks. All of these things help children to feel competent and powerful.

To counter children's fascination with commercialized superheroes, regularly include representations of strong and powerful people who are not gender stereotyped. Retell classroom activities as an adventure story with the children as characters. Create plots that reflect the tension of their developmental concerns—good and evil, strong and weak, acceptable and unacceptable.

Collaborate for Another Look at Your Environment and Routines

After working to incorporate the ideas of this chapter, ask a coworker to help you reassess your environment. Encourage her or him to use the checklist on pages 34–35 and walk around the different areas of your room, writing responses. Under "Already present," have your coworker list those items observed. Then meet together to brainstorm the items to add or eliminate under the "Goal" sections. Sometimes another person's perspective will clarify areas you have mastered or want to work on further. Collaboration enhances learning opportunities for you and your colleagues.

An Inspirational Story

The following story from a lab school director, Laurie S. Cornelius, was written in 1996 for the first edition of *Reflecting Children's Lives*. The work she and her colleagues did to create an outdoor play space—drawing on childhood memories, along with their decision to develop guidelines rather than rules—has created remarkable opportunities for children in their program. Notice their bold step in funding a teacher for the outdoor play space! In the intervening years, a new movement to reconnect children with nature has swept the country, with particular attention to rethinking designs for outdoor play spaces. Laurie's dream has continued to grow, as you will read in her postscript for this edition.

Our Dream Became Our Curriculum: A Story of an Outdoor Play Space

Laurie S. Cornelius, ECFE Lab School Director

A few years ago, our new child care center, a lab school for Clark College Early Childhood Education students in Vancouver, Washington, had a playground that was terribly inadequate and needed to be replaced. Basically, it was an empty play space with a few old and decaying structures that weren't safe. As these structures were torn down, my role as the director became finding the funding to create a new outdoor play space. It became a journey that was an emergent curriculum project for both adults and children. And it left us believing that we should never settle for less than our dreams.

Drawing on Our Own Childhood Memories

To develop our thinking about the kind of outdoor space we wanted to create, I decided to have parents and staff meet together to think about the play memories we had as children and experiences we thought were valuable enough to ensure for children. The group generated a huge list with many overlapping memories of playing outdoors. Play themes included risk taking, feeling powerful, constructing, hauling, transporting, digging, moving things to and from, having privacy, and having unstructured playing time with friends. We remembered different sounds and textures, seasonal changes, smells, and prickly, sandy, and muddy things. A source of water always meant endless possibilities for play.

As we looked at the list, we asked ourselves what elements were involved in each of these experiences. In other words, if you like to go and hide, then you need places in your environment to do that. If you like to build dams or forts, then you need water and rocks and logs to build with. If you like to lie under a tree, then you need shade trees. Some of our memories were of being raised on farms, jumping from bales and playing in the hay. We added to our list all the props and processes that would have to be built into an environment to provide for these childhood experiences.

I started working with Candy Bennett, a grant writer, who mentioned that federal block grant money designated for parks was available and asked if that was closer to the model we were after. We got involved in brainstorming to develop a concept that might be fundable by a broad spectrum of our community, including block grant monies. Our concept was that with upwards of 60 percent of children in child care, children aren't spending significant time in parks anymore. Instead, their time outdoors is spent in fenced-in playgrounds with few of the opportunities that a good park has to offer.

A significant shift in our thinking occurred as we started to look at child care and early childhood outdoor environments as parks. This moved us away from the school recess concept, with its limited view that gross-motor play was used for children to run and get their wiggles out so they will be better behaved inside. Returning again to our big list of childhood memories, we asked ourselves how we could use these elements to create a park concept inside a playground fence. As our thinking began to transform, so did our approach to fund-raising.

We knew that if we were to sell this concept to funders, we would have to utilize a buy-in that reflected deeper understandings than the usual idea of a climbing structure as a play space. I went through the phone book and found an architect, Ron Matela, who was available not only to walk through our empty outdoor play area with us, but also to willingly spend innumerable hours talking about our philosophy, the value of outdoor space, and the experiences of childhood.

Building on the Value of Risk Taking

One of our greatest challenges was to provide for risk taking while still keeping kids safe in our program. We wrestled with how to translate everybody's childhood memory of spending hours and hours outside, alone or with friends, exploring and having adventures with no adults around. All of our memories included taking risks that we knew wouldn't win adult approval. These risks often took on an air of mischief and misbehaving, but no one experienced any significant harm from them.

I strongly believe that taking risks is part of childhood, especially within the security of a family setting or child care program. If you aren't allowed to take risks as a child, you aren't likely to have good judgment about risk taking as an adult. Our center's evolving discussions about this strengthened our resolve to create a play space that would allow children to take risks and avoid letting our adult fears impede this. My sense is that often an adult watches an exploring or adventuresome child and gets fearful. This quickly translates into the adult either stopping the child in the name of protection or passing along that fear to the child.

Our discussions on providing for risk taking in the new play space design were intense, illuminating, and full of growth for all of us. We decided that we would need to keep our fear away from the children. We would allow ourselves to move into physical proximity where safety might be a strong concern. We would first try to use descriptive language with a child before intervening to stop something that had some particular risk involved. Our hope was that if we allowed a four-year-old child to fall when he rides his trike too fast around a curve, he won't have to experiment with this in a car when he's sixteen. We asked ourselves, "If a child tries to jump over a log and skins her knee, is that more dangerous than never understanding her body's capability as she grows and takes on more physical challenges?" I worry about a growing person's ability to self-impose needed limits if these limits have always been externally imposed by someone else.

What happens if our group care settings don't allow children the freedom to take risks and to feel capable of doing difficult things? How do they learn to make good judgments about whether something is safe if they have never experienced the consequences of their limitations? We have to allow children to experience little physical hurts so that they can learn natural consequences. In doing this, they start to develop a sense of their capabilities. They also have an experience of celebrating their success in trying something over and over again and finally learning to do it. These developmental understandings evolved out of our numerous adult discussions of our childhood memories. We decided we wanted the challenge of that emotional element to be in our planning design along with the physical challenges. The two go hand in hand.

Adapting What We Know Works Indoors

Another significant factor in the evolution of our outdoor planning was to learn from how we arranged the inside environment, something we're pretty good at. Rather than creating one big space to run around in, we decided to think in terms of learning centers and to create different outdoor areas for certain experiences. We had our list of childhood memories to help us define the kind of areas we wanted.

Indoors we typically use cupboards and shelving units to divide up space and create smaller group interest areas. How might we do that outdoors using materials more indigenous to the natural world? To plan for some of the elements we had been discussing, we began planting trees, bushes, and hedges, and adding rocks, logs, and stumps to naturally divide the space along these lines. We created a garden area, a quiet area, and several hill climbing and rolling areas. We created places to hide, dig in the sand, build structures, ride trikes, and make up dramas and games with friends. We considered the diverse sounds and textures of our childhoods in the out-of-doors—trees rustling, water gurgling, rocks crashing and splashing in a lake, tires thumping over wooden slats, branches and leaves and prickly things brushing against our skin. Was there a way to provide for these as we divided up the space?

We knew it was our responsibility to supervise children at all times, but we wanted to create spaces where kids had a sense of privacy and space away from adults—while still being visible to us. We started looking at how we could clump plantings of trees and bushes, create pits and hills so that the landscape would shape this feeling and provide a variety of clusters of smaller options for children's play. The decision about the few pieces of commercial equipment we purchased were based on how the equipment provided for social interaction and individualized creativity, along with large-motor skills.

Returning Again and Again to Our Philosophy

Perhaps the experience with our little covered bridge has taught us the most about putting our philosophy into practice. We originally designed the bridge as a place for children to ride their trikes across to hear a different kind of sound than on the cement. This idea came from our initial brain-storming session, and we thought it would be neat to make this part of the bike path that runs all around the play space. Then the children discovered new ways to use the bridge. Some of them began climbing over the railing to practice jumping over the rocks below. Adults nearly had heart attacks and wanted to quickly make rules so this couldn't happen.

This led to a discussion that resulted in the decision that no rules could be made quickly without really observing what the children were doing. Our observations would determine whether a rule we're inclined to make might be blocking some children's capabilities. If we make a general rule because a child may get hurt, what are we doing to all the children who can do this without the likelihood of getting hurt?

We finally asked ourselves, "Are the children who are trying to do this able to do it?" That was the best question that ever evolved, because it forced us to look more closely at who was really taking this risk. The children who weren't really competent at it yet were climbing over the railing, but they were hesitantly watching, not jumping. Other kids weren't even climbing over the railing, but just watching from the sidelines. When we observed, we saw children at all of these stages. A rule suitable for one of them would limit the development of others.

That was the first big discussion that challenged our philosophy. Soon after, we had a group of very competent five-year-olds who had been in gymnastics. They decided to climb up into the rafters of the bridge and hang upside down. So there they were, dangling upside down as children on trikes approached the bridge, heading toward them. More heart attacks for the adults. This didn't seem like a good idea. We were really worried. When we asked ourselves if the children were competent to do this, the answer was yes. When we asked if it was safe, the answer was no. We decided we needed a guideline.

We came up with the guideline that the children must find a partner who would close the bridge. Together they would figure out how to close it, and then the upside-down hanging would be safe enough. With guidelines rather than rules, we discovered a whole new level of possibilities for children to become problem solvers.

Using Portable Props for Play Themes

Another set of elements from our childhood memories involved construction and moveable props. We knew we had to have stuff to carry around and to do so on a variety of surfaces—grass, sand, concrete. Gradually we have collected big pieces of driftwood to add as props. Kids drag pieces around and often call to others to help with a heavy one. "We can't move this. Help us." It's so exciting to see. They have a plan, and it goes some place. One day a piece will be on the grass and another day in the sandpit.

I believe that by far the most important play props we have in the space are the rocks. We never would have considered that, but we knew from our memories that big rocks were important in building dams, building forts and pretend campfires, and blocking off streets for games. Because it was a universal in our memories of childhood, we decided on big rocks for hauling and building—rocks too big to throw but heavy enough to make hauling a worthwhile effort. The rocks move everywhere in our play space, with the exception of keeping them off the climber, where they could cause harm if dropped.

Another reason for including big rocks is because children feel powerful when they move big heavy things—and this is a key element of our philosophy. To create other opportunities for children to feel powerful, we also formed three tiers of hills so that children could get higher than the adults below. They get a sense of power from being able to scan the environment from above. Also, by simply planting bushes of different sizes and shapes, we made it possible for children to play hide-and-seek, peek-a-boo, or run-around-tag for hours. Tucking some of these bushes up closer to the fence, we've created a feeling of privacy, taking care to prune in some windows for visibility for the adults. This sense of independence is another component to helping children feel powerful.

Today our concept of needing ongoing planning of the outdoor space has evolved into funding a specific teacher for the job. She has her own storage space with supplies, and she plans curriculum for the outdoors in a way that parallels what other teachers do indoors—putting out new props for the children to discover and respond to, keeping an eye on the evolving play, and planning for emerging developmental interests and skills. When teachers and children come out into the space, she gives guidance to the adults about effective ways to supervise and work with guidelines. She's like a lead teacher for the out-of-doors, and classroom teachers team with her when they have ideas they want to bring outside. Getting this staff position would never have happened if we hadn't opened up our thinking and let our dreams become our curriculum.

This story is about creating visions for children and for adults. Boredom, fear, and hopelessness can eat us alive. We have to find ways of breaking loose from a sense of powerlessness, the feeling that things have changed and there's nothing we can do about it. I think we get caught in the reality of today and develop short-term solutions for things, forgetting to think about the long-term implications. Do the decisions we make for children in our programs today support the values we have for their childhood? Are our decisions developing capable people, or are they suppressing competency in order to make life easier or more convenient for adults?

The resources that emerged for our play space came about as a result of a vision that people believed in. Their vision was more than support for a project. The project was a concrete representation of a vision. The vision is the dream that we nurtured in each head; people translated that vision into specific action.

2010 Postscript: Looking Back and Looking Forward

It has been over a decade since we began our outdoor journey. Where are we today? I have many more questions and think most of the answers probably reside beyond the confines of our fences and require some bigger solutions. I've come to realize there are levels of understanding of how we plan and carry on the routines of our days with children.

On the surface is the daily care of an environment where our "to do" lists reside. Our play space weathers hard daily use. We spend a lot of time with our "to dos," such as management of equipment or coordinating schedules. A severe windstorm took out our favorite climbing tree, and a building project on lower campus broke our irrigation system one summer, damaging our plants. I'm reminded that life is not stagnant, nor can it be controlled. If our environments are of value to us, we must coexist with them, be attentive, and care for them, a requirement for all relationships. It is the relationship that must be nurtured. Our play space must be tended to, and all of us must be a part of the process. In addition to our seasonal outdoor curriculum, we've added a service day every spring when children, families, and staff come together to clean up and refurbish our outdoor space. When we plan and work together, we share a sense of pride and connection. We become stewards of a place. Children must be an inherent part of this process. However, we can't limit our awareness to surface details of the routines of our days. I worry we can get stuck in the routines of operations.

On a deeper level, I've asked myself, how do we create places both inside and out, that create the spirit of a place, of commitment and connection for ourselves, our children, and families? Intuitively I know the answer lies beyond creating environments limited to the narrow perspectives of standards and outcomes or even investigation and play. Children need meaningful roles in programs. We can't "teach to" children as if they are empty vessels. We must be with children as partners in their learning. It is an interactive process, as are our relationships with nature and with each other. It is the experience of this very relationship that will draw out passion, creativity, a desire to learn, and the discovery of the natural talents and gifts we can bring to the world.

I had the good fortune to attend the World Forum on Outdoor Nature Education, where early childhood educators, landscape architects, and community planners from twenty-six countries gathered to discuss the disconnect between children and nature and to examine efforts throughout the world to plan habitats and spaces for children. A powerful image I took away with me was that people worldwide have come to see that inadequate zoo environments cause unnatural stress behaviors in animals, so they have begun to create natural habitats where animals can thrive. Why do we see it with animals and not recognize this need for our children?

Where are we today? We are about to embark on another chapter of our journey. Fall 2010 marks the beginning of a three-phased project to build a new facility. We know the building will have a theme of transparency between the indoors and outdoors, a concept we tried to embody with our fences. We love the idea of bringing the world into the confines of our fences.

We will have an industrial kitchen off a large gathering room with a stage for our child-generated plays, and a big fireplace that will separate the parent/family library room from the big room. In trying to be transparent, a large peeled tree with branches will be in the vicinity of the fireplace between the two rooms. Rocks will carry over from the outdoors into the indoors in the floors. The interior dividers will become living walls (plants on walls) with willow gates (my hope).

We're adding a combined atelier and greenhouse that will have a portion of clear floor and roof where children can stand over a dry creek bed running down the hill (rocks). The rain runoff will filter down into the bed for a stream. Children will be able to stand over it and view it beneath their feet. We also are adding a hand pump for summer play and have talked about rain barrels. We are planning a garden maze with sculptures and an enchanted forest area. The toddler trike trail is going to be located in our kitchen herb garden.

Other thoughts we are working with: Beyond play, we are interested in habitats. Fences around individual age-defined programs are limiting. (Where fences are required, we are taking out all the chain-link fences and replacing them with wrought-iron ones). At the World Forum it was suggested that communities plan habitats and place children's programs on the edges. Parks and schools can grow beyond the concept of playgrounds. I have my eye beyond the confines of our fence but for now am focusing on our changing play space. Our families and some of our staff have changed, but we know we have inherited the passion and foundational work of those who came before us. We carry the responsibility of who we are today in the lives of children and families, realizing we do not own the program, as we will hand it to others in the future. We are stewards of the environment, of our program, and learning. Checklists and measures may need to exist, but we know learning and living go much deeper. My hope is that our play space will continue to evolve into a rich sensory experience where children play, live, and experience the responsibilities that come with being connected to the natural world, a "spirit of place."

▶ Share Your Reflections with Laurie

Write a letter to Laurie at LCorneliusReflect@gmail.com with your reflections on the process she went through to create a child-centered environment. Consider including your thoughts about the following:

- How do Laurie's vision, philosophy, and values about children and the environment influence her approach to planning for the environment?

- How did Laurie promote her vision and values with her staff, funders, and others in the community?

- What specific elements of Laurie's environment reflect children's lives and interests?

▶ *Practice What You've Learned*

Assess Your Environment, Rules, and Routines

Arrangement of Environment

Materials are visible, accessible, aesthetically organized, and inviting.

☐ Already present:

_____

_____

☐ Goal:

_____

_____

Loose parts (open-ended materials) are readily available inside and outside.

☐ Already present:

_____

_____

☐ Goal:

_____

_____

Diverse elements of texture, shape, and the natural world invite exploration and discovery.

☐ Already present:

_____

_____

☐ Goal:

_____

_____

Opportunities exist for transporting, combining, and transforming materials.

☐ Already present:

_____

_____

☐ Goal:

_____

_____

Visual images representing a range of roles and cultural expressions cultivate comfort with differences.

☐ Already present:

_____

_____

☐ Goal:

_____

_____

Representations of children's lives and interests appear around the room (photos, sketches, objects with stories).

☐ Already present:

_____

_____

☐ Goal:

_____

_____

Flexibility of space allows for expansion when many children are working in the same area.

☐ Already present:

_____

_____

☐ Goal:

_____

_____

Minimal restrictions exist to moving in and out of areas.

☐ Already present:

_____

_____

☐ Goal:

_____

_____

Places exist for physical activity and power.

☐ Already present:

_____

_____

☐ Goal:

_____

_____

Opportunities are available for adventure and risk taking.

☐ Already present:

_____

_____

☐ Goal:

_____

_____

Daily Routines

Large amount of time is available each day for continuous self-initiated play.

☐ Already present:

_____

_____

☐ Goal:

_____

_____

Minimal number of adult agendas interrupt children's play.

☐ Already present:

_____

_____

☐ Goal:

_____

_____

Flexibility in space and routines allows responding to children's interest.

☐ Already present:

_____

_____

☐ Goal:

_____

_____

Cleanup is not always required before a child moves to another area.

☐ Already present:

_____

_____

☐ Goal:

_____

_____

Play themes are incorporated into cleanup and group-time routines.

☐ Already present:

_____

_____

☐ Goal:

_____

_____

Little distinction exists between transitions and play.

☐ Already present:

_____

_____

☐ Goal:

_____

_____

Children negotiate taking turns with coaching from teachers (rather than teachers setting rigid time limits).

☐ Already present:

_____

_____

☐ Goal:

_____

_____

Notes about Your Current Environment

Looking over the goals you identified with your coworker, begin to make plans to achieve them.

What are your priorities? List them as next steps for yourself.

_____

_____

_____

_____

Where can you get the resources and support you need (e.g., coworkers, parents, community)?

_____

_____

_____

Guiding Children's Play and Learning

3

► Beginning Reflections

Daily life in an early childhood classroom is filled with the dynamic activities of the energetic bodies and lively minds of a group of young children. This hustle and bustle requires teachers to contend with the tensions of keeping the group on track while responding to the needs and interests of individual children.

How do we guide the hustle and bustle of a group of children while supporting the compelling needs and interests of individuals? Consider the following typical moment in an early childhood center.

It's the end of a busy morning in her preschool classroom, so teacher Janet begins moving around the room alerting children that it's almost time to clean up for snack and outside play. When she signals the end of playtime a few minutes later, most of the children begin to clean up and ready themselves. Wyatt and Chase, four-year-old boys, ignore their teacher's reminders and are still up in the loft looking at books, talking and laughing with obvious joy. Janet gives them a couple more gentle warnings, but they continue to ignore her. Finally, she calls up with a firm, loud voice and tells them they need to come down immediately. Chase and Wyatt stand up and begin shouting and chanting, "No, no, no, we won't come down; you can't make us. You aren't the boss of us!"

If you were teacher Janet what would you do?

☐ React sternly, marching up to the loft to physically bring the boys down.

☐ Warn the boys they will be put in time-out or lose the opportunity to play outside if they don't come down.

☐ Promise the boys you will give them something special if they cooperate with you and come down.

☐ Ignore them and move on with the rest of the group, giving the boys time to come down on their own.

☐ Other:

What about Techniques?

Working with young children can be challenging, as they don't follow organized routines and schedules easily, seemingly being more comfortable with their own natural rhythms and interests. Young children are learning how to regulate their own behavior and get along with others, so they often have conflicts that demand a teacher's time, attention, and patience.

Typical approaches to guidance and discipline offer early childhood teachers strategies and techniques to help children comply with rules and routines and learn the social skills that are necessary to work and play together in a group. There are many resources from which teachers can learn about group and behavior management techniques such as conflict resolution, redirection, time-out, behavior charts, and reward stickers. These approaches may work to control children's behavior in the moment and are more helpful than a teacher's frustrated reactions. But using these techniques robotically leads to meaningless quick fixes with no lasting value.

Goals for Guidance

Beyond getting children to behave, there are more important goals for guiding their play and learning. These child-centered goals help young children to

- understand the logic and value of rules and routines;
- see themselves as competent, contributing members of the group;
- understand and express their feelings and ideas (self-regulation);
- initiate their own activities and stay focused on their play and learning for long stretches of time; and
- see the value of working together and learn skills for collaboration.

Helping children to meet these goals is more complex than merely using guidance techniques to control behavior. It requires teachers to understand that challenging moments with children are opportunities to build toward these goals. Each moment of success or failure is a stepping-stone on the long road to self-regulation and learning social skills. In fact, if you think about it, adults continue to work on these goals throughout their lives. To truly help children learn self-control, initiative, and cooperation, teachers must incorporate the rhythm of childhood into the daily schedule and engage in more thoughtful interactions when conflicts occur.

Ensuring Time for Childhood

What are your best memories of *time* from your childhood? Did your life feel timeless or ruled by a schedule? Perhaps your days unfolded gloriously, with limited interruptions to your outdoor adventures and elaborate dramas, or maybe you had long stretches of time with a favorite adult who introduced you to the tools and skills of the real world.

Probably some of your unpleasant memories involve boredom while sitting still; waiting in lines; being rushed, interrupted, or punished; and having to follow instructions for something you had no interest in pursuing.

One of the greatest barriers to creating a child-centered program is the way many teachers organize children's time. Obviously routines and schedules are needed to avoid chaos and keep things running smoothly. Children benefit from predictability in their daily life. Yet, open, uninterrupted time is the foundation for rich childhood experiences. So how can you negotiate these tensions of accomplishing everything without regimenting or rushing children?

Child-Centered Schedules

A child-centered daily schedule isn't a free-for-all in which children do whatever they want all day. To the contrary, you play an active role in all aspects of the daily schedule, offering children free choice time as well as opportunities to lead or participate in activities that you initiate and organize. A child-centered schedule might look like this:

- The routines for daily living and learning happen in the same sequence each day, but the amount of time for each routine is based on the children's rhythms and interests.

- A large amount of time is available each day for children's self-initiated play within an environment carefully planned by the teacher. (Remember, research shows that children require more than thirty minutes of sustained, engaged, self-initiated play for complex play to emerge.)

- Cleanup is not always required before a child moves to another area, in order to help children learn to sustain their attention.

- The teacher reorders the environment during child-initiated play to help maintain order and the children's focus.

- The teacher coaches children to negotiate taking turns rather than setting rigid time limits.

- Opportunities exist throughout the day when children are invited to participate in activities initiated and led by the teacher. These activities fully involve the children through use of materials and active engagement with the teacher and each other.

- Teacher-directed instruction when children have to sit, wait, and listen with no active involvement is limited.

Sample Flexible Daily Schedule

7:00–9:00 arrival, reading, eating, playing with friends

9:00–9:20 group gathering, stories, singing, sharing, planning

9:20–11:45 choice of interest areas, project work, both indoors and ample time outdoors

11:45–12:15 cleanup, preparation for lunch

To create a calm atmosphere and support individual children's needs, organize your daily schedule around the rhythms of childhood, not the clock.

Who Has the Power?

As an adult, you hold all the power over the lives of the young children. You control the time and the routines. You are bigger and have more experiences, words, and abilities. You are in charge of the lights, the food, and the toys and activities that are available to children. You decide what to pay attention to and how you will respond. True, you may struggle with the dynamics of your group and with individual children. You may feel pressured by family concerns or expectations from supervisors and early learning standards. With all the demands on you, at times you may be the one who feels powerless.

In reality, you have the power in the moment-to-moment interactions with children that matter the most. The way you use your power has a huge impact on children's daily experiences and your own joy in your work.

The Latin root of the word power means "to be able." Having power means having the capacity to make a difference, to have worth or value.

Your goal for both you and the children should be to have the power to make a difference and feel valued. You can use your power to support children's abilities and feelings of self-worth. Yet you must always be aware that your power can also easily oppress children, undermining their instinctive goals for autonomy and competence. Using your power on behalf of children requires continuous reflection and negotiation.

Elizabeth Jones and Eve Trook (1983) identified the kinds of power adults use with children. Studying the different kinds of power can help you understand the best ways to use your power with children.

Power On

Adults use Power On to prevent or stop children from their pursuits and interests. This kind of power often oppresses children, as they feel powerless and unable to act on their own, which can negatively impact their feelings of self-worth. The appropriate time to use this kind of power with children is when their actions will result in

- hurting themselves;
- hurting others; or
- damaging materials or property.

On the surface, choices involving the use of power around safety issues and rules may appear to be easy decisions. If a child is going to get hurt, hurt someone else, or destroy something, you must immediately stop the behavior. Children need to take safe risks, however, to feel competent and develop self-esteem. You should be thoughtful, not just reactive, when deciding how and when to use Power On.

Read the following two scenarios that involve the use of Power On. After reading them, reflect on the behaviors of the teachers. Can you see how one teacher is using her power on behalf of the children and the other is undermining the child's self-worth?

Two-year-old Ariel is trying to climb up the front of his high chair. As he reaches for the tray, the chair begins to fall over. Teacher Kamisha immediately grabs him by the arm and scoops him up as the chair tumbles over. Ariel screams in shock and begins to cry. Kamisha says gently, "Ariel, you are such a busy climber these days. But look. See how the chair fell over? If I didn't grab you, you would fall down and get hurt. I'm sorry if I scared you."

Four-year-old Gemma runs in from the playground, excited to tell her teacher about the deep hole she has dug in the sand. Teacher Morgan immediately takes Gemma's hand and leads her back outside as she sternly says, "Gemma, you know we don't run in the classroom. It's not safe. It's outside time now, and you need to stay outdoors so the teachers know where you are." When Gemma protests, Morgan says, "I don't want any complaining. You need to follow the rules or you'll be put in time-out."

Power For

Adults use Power For in behalf of children's power through coaching and scaffolding. Using Power For children is what makes teaching an art and a science, not just a bag of tricks and strategies. Rather than being the "preschool police," jumping in to prevent or solve problems, you use your adult wisdom, skills, and knowledge to help children develop their own understandings and competence. You continually decide between when to step in and offer support and when to allow children to figure things out for themselves.

Now read the next two scenarios that demonstrate the use of Power For. After reading them, think about the differences between Power On and Power For. How do you think children experience the different ways teachers use their power?

Two-year-old Shay wants to take her sweater off. Teacher Eric encourages her to do it herself. Shay struggles mightily when she can't get the sweater over her head. Eric watches, offering encouragement. "Keep trying, Shay;

you've almost got it." Her struggle continues a bit longer, and Eric says, "I'll help by pulling on your sleeve here so you can have more wiggle room." His small action is a scaffold for her and leads to success as Shay pulls the sweater off. "Yeah, you worked hard, and you did it, Shay!" Eric announces as Shay smiles proudly.

Four-year-old Rafael has been trying to construct a tall, narrow tower with the blocks. The tower has tipped over several times because Rafael has been stacking the blocks off center and out of balance. After the fifth try, Rafael complains to his teacher. "I can't get this to stay up." Teacher Michele says, "I've been watching you working hard at this. Let me show you what I noticed. When you stack the blocks, some of them are hanging off the edge of each other, and the higher you build like that the tippier the tower becomes." She demonstrates his method, and the blocks tumble. "Let me show you what I think might work. If you put each block on top of the other so no edges are hanging over, they will have the balance to stay up." Rafael uses Michele's coaching, and this time his tower stays up. "I did it!" he announces triumphantly.

Power With

Adults use Power With side by side with children, sharing and allowing, rather than guiding behavior or activities. Many teachers find joy in diving in and playing right along with the children. This can be a fun, empowering experience for children as they become your peers, sharing power through the exchange of ideas and actions. Children can also learn useful social skills through playing with their teacher. As an adult, you have to monitor yourself so that you don't get so carried away in the fun of the play that you inadvertently take over and it becomes more of a Power On than a Power With situation.

Here's a scenario of a teacher using Power With.

Teacher Alexis has joined the group of three-year-olds in the rowboat on the playground. "Where are we going today?" she asks. "To the moon," the children shout together. "Okay, time for liftoff. I see stars all around me. It's so beautiful," Teacher Alexis says with wonder in her voice. "I see clouds!" one of the children offers. "I see space," says another. The drama continues with teacher and children sharing their imaginations on their way to the moon.

Look Closer at Challenging Behaviors

Study the following list of typical situations in an early childhood setting and reflect on how you might approach these challenges if you were the teacher:

- Four-year-olds Brianna and Nicole have been intently playing together all morning in the doll corner when another child, Elise, comes over and asks to join in. "You can't play with us. We already have a mommy and a baby. You're not our friend. Go away!" they tell her.

- Barely three-years-olds Josh and Eli are in the sandbox gleefully throwing shovels full of sand at each other.

- James wasn't ready to come in from outdoor playtime. As he enters the room, he moves around to the different play areas purposefully tipping over chairs and knocking toys off of the shelves.

- Two-year-old Tavon grabs the ball that eighteen-month-old Caleb is playing with. When Caleb starts to scream, Tavon bites him.

- You've told a group of four-year-old boys several times to stop climbing a tree, but when you look over, they are sitting high up in the tree branches.

- Eleven-month-old Serena throws her bowl of oatmeal off the table and onto the floor, laughing as it splatters everywhere.

Beyond Behavior Management

Young children are in the process of developing initiative to explore their world and practice new skills. They are learning how to regulate their own behavior and get along with others. They often behave in ways that teachers find challenging. How do you maintain a child-centered focus when the children's focus results in behaviors that may cause disruptions and hurt (or danger) to themselves and others? Your task is to work through these moments and respond purposefully, offering support and understanding. The following sections provide guidelines that can help you be more prepared with thoughtful responses to the everyday challenges you face, small and large.

Know Your Hot Buttons

Your background, values, and life experiences have a huge impact on how you respond to challenging moments with children. Recognizing the behaviors and situations with children that "push your buttons" can help you mediate your responses. Some of the things that happened to you as a child and how the adults in your life responded have become a part of your emotional makeup. If you reflect on these experiences, you come to see that the strong feelings you are having at a given moment may be coming from somewhere other than the behavior of the children you are teaching.

When you know yourself, you respond more thoughtfully to children rather than reacting from unexamined emotions. You can separate your feelings and experiences from the children's behavior and respond calmly with a clear mind. Revisit the list of Challenging Behaviors on pages 82–83 and use the following questions to think through your reactions. This self-reflection will help you get to know yourself in such moments and identify your "hot spots."

- How am I reacting to this situation? What actions would I want to take immediately?

- What experiences from my own childhood and the way challenging behaviors were handled may be influencing my reactions?

- How are my beliefs and values influencing my response to this situation and why?

With more self-awareness, you can become more intentional in your responses, considering the child's perspective as you decide what to say and do.

What Child Do You See?

When teachers believe that children are capable of learning, they will take the time to help children reach their full potential.

Your perception of children is fundamental to how you respond to challenging moments. If you consider children to be competent and believe that their behavior has an important purpose that should be respected, you will respond with patience and coaching. If you see children as naughty or lacking control, then you will likely take less time to support children in solving problems for themselves. You can practice transforming your view of children so when these moments arise, you bring, as the educators of Reggio Emilia say, "a strong image of the child" to your response.

Here is an example of contrasting views of the same behavior in children.

Negative View	Competent View
Have no idea of what is safe	Are energetic explorers, tireless experimenters, dedicated scientists
Lack patience	Are eager to learn from every experience and interaction they have
Cannot keep their hands off of things	Are figuring out how to control their behavior and look after themselves, others, and the world around them
Have temper tantrums	Are moving from dependence to independence

Meet Up with Children's Hearts and Minds, Not Their Behaviors

To help you transform your view of children, look beyond their behavior. Bring a strong understanding of their skills and competence to your interactions with children. When you consider the child's point of view, your response will reflect and support their ideas and feelings. Return again to the list of Challenging Behaviors on pages 82–83. Practice connecting with the children's hearts and minds by answering the following questions about each of the situations:

- What is on the child's mind in this moment? What is she trying to accomplish?

- What are the feelings underneath this behavior? How can I put myself in the child's shoes to see this from his point of view? What touches my heart as I consider this child's feelings?

- What is underneath the behavior that indicates the child knows how to express personal ideas and feelings and accomplish goals?

- What from my own life can I relate to this situation?

Recognize Children's Eagerness for Relationships

Learning how to make friends and get along with others are important outcomes for children in early childhood programs. In the "real world," children must learn how to meet their own needs while at the same time cooperating, communicating, and negotiating with others. This is the foundation of a democratic society. Young children's efforts at forming friendships offer them some of the most satisfying moments and also some of the most difficult struggles.

Children thrive on relationships with others. Children confirm an intuitive desire in human beings to reach out and support one another from the day they are born. Yet often the emphasis in teachers' work is children's inability to get along with each other. Teachers try to learn as many skills and techniques as they can to manage conflicts, continually working to prevent and solve children's problems for them.

Instead, imagine seeing children as already possessing the capacity for developing relationships and your role as helping them use this innate ability. If you carry this view of children throughout your work, you will recognize children's huge capacity for offering support and comfort, as well as accepting and benefiting from the gifts of friendship offered by others. Rather than viewing their struggles with each other as negative, you can recognize that even children's most challenging

behaviors reveal that they are eager to connect and are genuinely fascinated with one another's words, ideas, and actions.

If you can come to the powerful realization that children have the
capacity and desire for deep connections, then you will support and
coach them to grow into their best selves. But transforming your view
of children's challenging behaviors in their efforts to connect with others is no easy task. It becomes even more daunting when you are faced
with the realities of negotiating daily life with a large group of young
children. Use the following principles to cultivate your ongoing practice
to see children's eagerness for relationships.

Notice and Marvel at Children's Positive Interactions with Each Other

Noticing the moments when children have positive interactions with
each other will reinforce your understanding that all children have
the capacity for empathy and kindness; they are eager to play a role in

helping others. When you carry this knowledge, you will take the time to support children to negotiate their own conflicts and strengthen their ability to collaborate. Use the following questions to focus your observations on children's positive interactions:

- What specific things do children do and say that indicate they are connecting with each other and building relationships?

- How do they use the objects or materials in their play to communicate their ideas?

- What do the children do and say to successfully resolve their differences or conflicts?

Coach Children to Offer Their Ideas and Competence

As you observe children's skills and competencies, encourage them to show what they know and what they can do. When children share their ideas and teach others, they develop a view of themselves as important, contributing members of the group. They also come to view their peers as resources and begin to understand the value of collaboration.

Reinforce Children's Positive Social Interactions

Tell stories and create homemade books with photos showing the children's positive social interactions and successful conflict negotiations. Use words and photos that acknowledge the powerful, conflicting feelings children may have in these moments of relating to each other. Also include concrete images that illustrate their success in getting along and developing new friendships. Studying these books with children reinforces the helpful ways they already know about working together and reminds them how to use these positive behaviors more with each other.

Consider the Recursive Cycle of Development

During your time as a teacher, you will probably come to know many young children with life struggles leading to behaviors that challenge you and disrupt the experience of the group. Your job isn't to try and "fix" these children, but instead to help them develop satisfying relationships with others and see themselves as important contributors to the group. Often you will need to seek help from others to support you in your work with challenging behaviors. The most important gift you can offer these children is an understanding that underneath their challenging behavior is a deep desire for connections with others.

In writing about the recursive cycle, Lilian Katz (1986) proposes that children who use negative behaviors in social situations receive negative responses from both adults and children, which in turn provoke more negative behaviors from them, leading to still more negative responses. This cycle continues on and on, feeding the child's troubled sense of self and reinforcing negative behaviors. Katz's observations can inspire you to think about the power and responsibility you have to break this cycle for these children.

An effective way to break the cycle is to transform your view of children's challenging behaviors. When you seek children's points of view and strive to understand how their behaviors reveal a deep desire and eagerness for relationships, you won't give up on them. You will take the time and use your skills and knowledge to support children in developing the nourishing friendships they deserve. There is no more important or rewarding work than this.

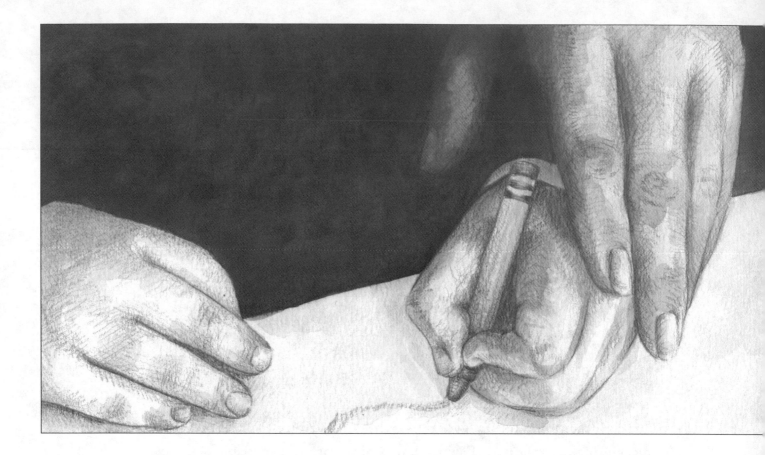

An Inspirational Story

As you read the following story, notice how teacher-trainer Christina Aubel uses her power with the children. What is her image of children? How is the approach she is taking with Chelsea's teacher similar to how she hopes the teacher will guide Chelsea?

Chelsea's Teacher

Christina Aubel, Mentor Teacher

I arrived earlier than usual on a hot summer day and found the preschool teacher with only three children. I squinted into the shade-drawn room. The children ran toward me calling, "Christina!" I hugged each child and smiled at the teacher.

"Only three children?" I asked.

"The others will be here soon," she replied.

We looked at each other as if searching for a place to begin. I remember that same uncertainty when a trainer would enter my classroom, polished and prepared to change me. All these years later, I'm still practicing my listening skills. So I wait for a cue from the teacher before speaking.

We sat across from one another in child-sized chairs at a child-sized table. The three children in the classroom visited with each other nearby. "I think I'm too patient with the children," the teacher sighed as she folded towels fresh from the dryer.

Curious, I leaned forward. This was the most reflective she'd been with me in the four months I've worked with her, and I didn't want to miss this opportunity. As I pondered how or if I should respond given that children were in the room, the door from the outside flung open and in tumbled children, mothers, and sunshine. In the lead was three-year-old Chelsea, the ponytail spiked high on her head bouncing slightly with each step. She stopped for a moment. This smiling, stubborn rebel of a girl wearing white sandals, pink shorts, and a white and pink flowery top surveyed her classroom then ran after her mother, who had walked into the director's office.

The "patient teacher" called after Chelsea. When she did not respond, the teacher marched out, returning with the wailing child. "Time-out," the teacher said, sitting Chelsea at the wall. Bending over the child, she said firmly, "You may not leave the classroom." A few minutes later the teacher allowed Chelsea to join the class. As I watched the other children interact, I heard another, "Time-out!" I turned to see Chelsea, head down, seated at the wall once more. I noted it had been only ten minutes since this child had bounced into the classroom.

It was noon before the teacher and I were able to continue our morning conversation. We sat at the same table and in the same chairs while the children settled into naptime. We had fifteen minutes until her lunch break.

I whispered, "So you were saying you think you're too patient?"

She stated that when she first came to work at this center she had given the children many chances, but they didn't listen and didn't do what she asked, so now she uses time-out right away.

I wondered how to respond. "Time-out is tricky, especially if you use it a lot. Do you think it's working?"

She shrugged her shoulders.

I looked at the clock and then dove in, "I'm concerned that if Chelsea spends so much of the day against the wall, she's going to feel really bad and believe she is bad. It's our job to educate her—not police her. Let's catch her when she's doing the thing, the positive behavior, you want to see—let's catch her doing that. Let's tell her how proud we are of her and how proud she must be of herself."

The teacher wasn't aware that earlier I'd heard her say to Chelsea she would have to tell Chelsea's mother that she hadn't listened today.

I said to the teacher, "What if at the end of each day you tell Chelsea's mother the thing she's done well that day—even if it's just one thing? And what if you say it in front of Chelsea—how do you think this child will feel?"

I searched the teacher's eyes for a hint of acknowledgment. I waited then continued, "What if the director walked in right now and I said to her you must be so proud to have a teacher of this quality in your center." Her face lit up. I continued, "Chelsea's stubbornness—that determination, that knowing what she wants—will serve her well when she's an adult. She could be the president of a company. It's hard for us now, but it's hard for her too. The question for us to answer is, how can we help her be successful?"

The teacher and I turned to watch Chelsea sleeping that elegant child sleep. The teacher whispered worriedly, "But she tears up her papers and crushes them into a ball!" She demonstrated a wild tearing and crushing motion, asking, "Should I let her do that?"

The teacher cared. I could see it in her eyes. I wondered what words I could say to help and give her guidance.

I suggested, "They're Chelsea's papers. You might ask her, 'How can I help you? I'm sorry you ripped up your paper. If you decide to save it, I can give you some tape, or we can smooth it out and put it in your cubby.'" Then I reminded her of an occurrence a few days prior when Chelsea found success.

That day the teacher called all the children to a table to work on writing their numbers. She held up a work sheet illustrated with the number 9 and nine small rabbits. She pointed to each rabbit, and the children counted in unison. She passed out a sheet to every child except Chelsea and two other three-year-olds. Instead of the rabbits, she them gave a ditto with an illustration of the number 1 and one ice cream cone. Chelsea struggled to hold her crayon. Then, seeing that some other children were able to trace their numbers, she threw her crayon across the table, nearly hitting me. She held her head down and her lips tight as tears formed. I asked her if I could help. Eyebrows furrowed, she nodded yes, so I stood behind her and took her hand. Her fingers tensed but then relaxed to let me arrange them around the crayon. With my hand guiding hers, we traced the number 1. As we traced, I said, "Up and down." Chelsea and I traced the number 1, singing "up, down, up, down," until she was on her own. The other children joined in the song.

"Done!" Chelsea exclaimed as she dropped her crayon and jetted toward the puzzles.

By the time I finished recalling the story about Chelsea and the number 1, it was almost 12:15, and the teacher needed to make certain the children were settled before leaving for lunch. I helped her with a child who was off his mat and playing with the Legos. My mind raced to find ideas and words the teacher could take to consider further.

I began, "The question we must always ask ourselves is, how can we give children opportunities to think, problem solve, and learn self-control. If we continually put children in time-out, then what is it that we are teaching them? What are they learning? It seems to me you are doing all the thinking, and all Chelsea is doing is crying."

The tilt of her head told me she was considering these ideas. We looked at each other and then the clock. It was 12:16, and she gathered her things and clocked out.

"See you next time," I said.

She smiled at me slightly, then headed into the sunshine.

I sighed and thought to myself, "Time-outs this time; work sheets another time."

Share Your Reflections with Christina

Write a letter to Christina at CAubelReflect@gmail.com with your reflections on how she was coaching the teacher about guiding children's behavior. Consider including your thoughts about the following:

- What is Christina's view of children, and how does her view impact how she coaches the teacher?
- What is the teacher's view of Chelsea, and how is this different from Christina's view?
- If you were the teacher Christina was working with, how would you respond?

▸ *Practice What You've Learned*

Notes about Your Approach to Guiding Behavior and Supporting Relationships

Reflect on what you have read in this chapter about guiding behavior, power, and supporting relationships. The following questions can help you to focus your thinking. Use the space provided to jot down your reflections.

How does your use of time and classroom routines reflect the children's rhythms and interests?

_____

_____

_____

_____

_____

What kind of power do you use most often with children? What changes would you like to make?

_____

_____

_____

_____

_____

_____

What are your "hot buttons" in challenging moments with children? How can you strengthen your ability to respond to situations with a calm, clear mind?

_____

_____

_____

_____

_____

_____

_____

What view do you have of the children's skills and competencies? In what ways do you need to transform your view of children to see them in a more positive light?

_____

_____

_____

_____

_____

_____

_____

What is your view of children's ability to resolve conflicts and work collaboratively? How will you strengthen your ability to support their social competence?

_____

_____

_____

_____

_____

_____

_____

Putting the Child Back in DAP

▶ Beginning Reflections

When you hear the term *developmentally appropriate practice,* what comes to mind?

Do you think of school readiness activities and lesson plans that have been watered down to work better for younger children? Or is your mental image one of children spending long periods of time engrossed in building elaborate structures with blocks with you commenting on the math concepts you see involved? Is it childhood or school readiness that guides your thinking when planning curriculum?

Record your thoughts here:

_____

_____

_____

_____

_____

_____

_____

Teacher's Ideas versus Child's Interest

In the early years of our profession's publications and professional discourse about developmentally appropriate practice (DAP), some teachers mistakenly thought it was a curriculum. DAP is not a curriculum in and of itself. It is a set of principles and guidelines for teaching practices that ensure young children learn and develop to their fullest potential in meaningful ways. These DAP guidelines are continually critiqued, debated, and revised to reflect current research and experience within the profession. Along with DAP, new professional language is calling for "developmentally effective approaches." Overall, the task for teachers in using the DAP guidelines is to respond to and plan for children's individual development and learning within the cultural context of each child's family and community.

Keeping the definition of DAP in mind, read through the curriculum plans below from two teachers, Ron and Corrine. Which do you think represents developmentally appropriate practice?

Ron's Color-of-the-Week Curriculum

Ron is planning curriculum activities to teach children their colors. He has been looking through activity books for ideas he thinks the children will like. For each week in September, Ron will teach a "color of the week." Here are some of the activities he has planned for each color:

- Mix the color of the week for painting at the easel.
- Have a collage art project with different shapes of that color to glue.
- Label the colors in a bulletin board display.
- Play "Can you find something of this color?"
- Put selected pieces from the color lotto game out on the table.
- Dismiss the children by the colors they are wearing.

Corrine's Paint-Mixing Color Curriculum

All week Corrine has observed four-year-old Lena engaged in pouring
and stirring paint in the containers at the art table. Noting this interest,
Corrine arranges for Lena to discover something new today. Corrine sets
out only red and blue paint. Going to the easel, Lena takes a brush and
makes a few strokes of red on her paper. Next she uses the blue to paint
a few letters in her name. Putting the brush again in the red paint and
sweeping it across the paper, she exclaims, "Look, it's changing!"

Corrine responds with a smile, "You mix it; it changes." Lena begins
pouring the red paint into the blue and stirring it with her brush. She
calls out her understanding. "Corrine, it's all red-blue." Suddenly a
moment of new understanding is visible on Lena's face and in her voice
as she bursts out with, "Look, Corrine, now it's changing to purple!"

Observation Is the Heart of the Matter

When you compare Ron's and Corrine's color curriculums, you discover the foundation of DAP—planning from close observation and careful analysis of children rather than centering on lessons from activity books. Ron's curriculum centers on his ideas and thinking—a teacher-centered curriculum. Corrine's curriculum focuses on Lena's interests—a child-centered curriculum.

The following table compares and contrasts these two curriculums.

Ron's Color Curriculum	Corrine's Color Curriculum
Ideas for curriculum come from books and what the teacher wants the children to learn.	Observation of children's interests and activities is the basis for curriculum ideas.
The focus is on exposing children to different colors and learning color names.	The focus is on a child's discovery and exploration that will lead to deeper interests and understandings of how colors are created.
The curriculum's direction and desired outcomes are predetermined by the teacher. Children perform teacher-planned activities with little understanding or even interest in why.	Curriculum direction is set by the child. The teacher focuses desired outcomes on the child's initiative as she pursues things she wants to understand.
The curriculum covers the names and recognition of four colors.	The curriculum unfolds as the child's interest in mixing colors is discovered and sustained, with teacher responses and planning that build in possibilities for the child to acquire deeper understandings.

Observation is the heart of child-centered emergent curriculum planning. Observing children will teach you a great deal about child development. It will help you identify additional skills you might want to learn. You will become resourceful, imaginative, and more curious about children. You will remember why you love this work.

Skills Required for a Child-Centered Curriculum

Learning to be an observer, gathering data about who the children are— their interests, questions, strengths, and challenges—constitutes the starting point for building a child-centered curriculum. Observation is a critical tool for ongoing assessment, planning, and responses to children.

Observing children is both an art and a skill. Observation skills involve an objective, detailed collection of data and an eye for the meaning and richness of each child's play and learning experience.

The most difficult challenge of observing is to recognize your own perspective, bias, and filters, which prevent you from describing the objective details of what you are seeing. When observing, adults tend to quickly interpret situations and come to conclusions before gathering data and analyzing it objectively.

Your background, life experiences, values, and expectations all influence how you filter observations and other information. To observe more objectively, you must practice suspending your filters and initial interpretations of what you are seeing.

Practice Learning to Observe

You can practice noting the difference between descriptive observations and interpretations.

Use photos or find a magazine photograph of children and adults involved in some kind of activity. Quickly write a list of statements about what you see in the photograph. Read through your list. Write a *D* next to the words and statements that are specific descriptions of what is in the picture. These are usually the elements of a situation that most people would identify and agree upon.

Next, look for statements you wrote that are interpretations of the scene, rather than more objective descriptions. Put an *I* next to these. These are conclusions based on your own filters or subconscious cues picked up from the scene. For more direction, look at the chart below and note the difference.

Descriptive Data: The Skill of Observation	Interpretations: The Art of Observing
One adult, one child, and one baby	A family: a mom with her two children
The adult is holding the baby on her lap, looking down at the child, smiling.	The mom thinks her baby is so cute.
The child is standing behind the adult with her hands covering the adult's eyes.	The child is jealous because the mom is paying too much attention to the baby.

Under the "Descriptive Data" column, only observable facts are noted. This data is important to distinguish from assumptions you might be making. The data in the "Interpretations" column should be based on the specific details of observable facts, not assumptions. As you look at the chart again, notice how the observer could be jumping to conclusions without adequate data for her interpretations.

Questions for Analyzing Observation Notes

The following questions can guide you in developing the art of observation:

- What did I specifically see that led me to make these statements?

- Are there subtle cues (e.g., body posture, facial expressions, clothing, or colors) that influenced my thinking?

- Are my statements based on any filters from my own experience, background, or values?

Your observation notes are not necessarily wrong, nor do you want to ignore them. In fact, interpreting your observations is the heart (and art) of observation. Interpreting descriptive data and underlying cues becomes the foundation of child-centered planning.

The goal is to be as objective as possible. You want to be aware of your filters and biases and how they influence the way you informally collect data (information) about children. Each response and plan you make should be based on what you understand about the child and your own values and goals for the situation.

Questions to Guide Interpretation and Planning

- What did you specifically see?

- How would you describe this experience from the child's point of view?

- What does this child know how to do?

- What does this child find frustrating?

- How does this child feel about herself or himself?

- What do you think is most significant here and why?

Ask yourself repeatedly, "What did I *specifically* see?" Finding descriptive details is a critical skill in the observation process. Record your descriptions and review them. When you notice you have made an overly general statement, ask yourself, "What did I specifically see that makes me say that?" Find ways to back up your statements with descriptive data.

For example, if you observed, "The child was angry," try to answer the question, "What did I specifically see that made me think he was angry?" Specific descriptions related to anger might be, "I saw the child frown, stomp his feet, and yell."

Initially, try to avoid drawing any conclusions so you can practice the skill of gathering details with clues and information before you make interpretations and plans. As you move to the art of interpretation, put yourself in the children's shoes and consider what you have just seen through their eyes.

To understand the children's point of view, consider the following:

- What are they trying to do in their play?

- What experiences, knowledge, and skills are they building on?

- What questions, inventions, or problems are they encountering?

- What do they find meaningful? Frustrating? Challenging?

- What might they want from you or their playmates?

Observation and Recording Skills

To enhance your skill as an observer in collecting data, use the following guidelines.

Objectivity

Record objective details; avoid making initial judgments or broad generalizations. Objective recording strives to be noninterpretive. Saying, "The boys were much too noisy and out of control," interprets the meaning of a behavior that isn't specifically described. In contrast, "During cleanup Jonathan and Jason yelled across the room at each other, arguing as to who was the last to play with the blocks" describes the behavior labeled as "too noisy and out of control." A more detailed description allows you to assess the context and any personal filters that might be influencing your interpretation. The best way to strive for objectivity is by gaining awareness of your own subjectivity and then seeking perspectives from others.

Specificity

Record specific details regarding the number of children and adults involved in an activity, the amount and kind of materials available, the passage of time, and other relevant objective factors. This provides detail to the context of the observation.

Directness

Record direct quotes. Although this is a difficult skill to master, it is very useful when analyzing observation notes. For instance, a note that includes the sentence, "Jason said, 'I was playing with that first,'" indicates that the child has language skills for resolving conflicts.

Completeness

Record observations of incidents from beginning to end. A complete recording describes the setting, who was involved, what action occurred, what the reaction was, and how the incident occurred.

Mood Clues

Record mood clues, such as tone of voice, facial expressions, body posture, hand gestures, and other nonverbal body clues. Including mood clues in written observations helps you make inferences about the social and emotional climate of a situation.

Practice Interpreting Observations

Practice your observation skills. Read the following observation description. Then write down each sentence from it under one of the two headings on the next page.

> Derek is standing at the sand table, playing with large plastic dinosaurs. He digs in the sand, burying one of the plastic dinosaurs and a dinosaur skeleton. "This one has been dead a long time," he says, pointing to the skeleton dinosaur. "This one isn't dead yet," he says, smiling, "I'd better not bury it."
>
> Derek grabs a tiny shovel and pickax and begins uncovering each of the dinosaurs he buried. Is he exploring something about death? He seems to understand that bones are what is left after one dies.
>
> He digs up the large plastic dinosaur and starts putting sand down its big open mouth. "Here, you better eat your vegetables. I'm going to fill you all up with vegetables," he says, filling the dinosaur with sand. "I need a funnel to fill him up." He probably thinks that it will take less time to fill up the dinosaur with a funnel. Derek is a very smart child. His play is sophisticated.

Descriptions

Interpretations/Questions/ Curiosities

_____

_____

_____

_____

_____

_____

_____

_____

_____

_____

_____

_____

_____

_____

_____

_____

_____

_____

Next, ask yourself these questions:

What does Derek know how to do? Be specific.

_____

_____

_____

_____

What does he find frustrating? Add any specific indicators.

_____

_____

_____

_____

How does he feel about himself? What clues tell you this?

_____

_____

_____

_____

What is the essence of this experience for Derek? Name its meaning or theme in a phrase.

_____

_____

_____

_____

A Closer Look

The teacher who wrote the observation of Derek used many descriptive statements, including direct quotations of what he said. With these direct statements, she had data that led her to interpret that Derek understood some aspects of death and is exploring more. She had less than adequate information here to support the interpretations of the last two sentences.

Perhaps her assessment that Derek is smart and a sophisticated player is built on an accumulation of observations. If so, she could strengthen the validity of these interpretative statements by making reference to how this observation is consistent with others in the past.

Becoming a skilled observer takes practice. On page 112, you'll find a blank form to copy and use. Spend fifteen to thirty minutes observing a child or small group of children to give you data to interpret and then use for curriculum planning. Start by recording your descriptions on the top part of the page, noting things you specifically observe. At the end of your observation period, review what you've written and then fill in the Interpretations section at the bottom. Again, ask yourself the following questions:

- [ ] What are they trying to do in their play?
- [ ] What experiences, knowledge, and skill are they building on?
- [ ] What questions, inventions, or problems are they encountering?
- [ ] What do they find meaningful? Frustrating? Challenging?
- [ ] What might they want from you or their playmates?

Program Observations

Observation setting: _____

Time and date of observation: _____

Observer: _____

Descriptions

_____

_____

_____

_____

_____

_____

_____

Interpretations/Questions/Curiosities

_____

_____

_____

_____

_____

_____

_____

_____

_____

Developing an Eye for Complex Play in Your Program

Another way to practice your observation skills for developing appropriate curriculum practice is to look for key elements of children's play. These will alert you to the children's developmental process and the emerging academic concepts they are exploring. Observe the children, and ask yourself the following questions to determine whether they are involved in productive, complex play. If any of these elements are missing, you can develop goals for yourself to provide them.

Are the children . . .

☐ making props for their own play?

Observations:

_____

_____

☐ engaging peers and/or adults in dramatic play?

Observations:

_____

_____

☐ transforming space and material to meet their needs?

Observations:

_____

_____

☐ negotiating roles and problems with their peers?

Observations:

_____

_____

☐ continuing thematic play from day to day?

Observations:

_____

_____

☐ using special vocabulary with increasingly complex sentence structure?

Observations:

_____

_____

☐ exploring understandings of academic learning domains (e.g., literacy, science, math)?

Observations:

_____

_____

An Inspirational Story

As you read Kristie L. Norwood's story of her work in an urban Head Start program, notice how she began to change her mind-set after studying her observations. Her observations helped her to see a child's passion for learning, as well as recognize what he already knew. This allowed her to follow his lead as she guided his project work.

Igniting a Passion for Learning through Uncovering Children's Interest

Kristie L. Norwood, Head Start Education Coordinator

When I talk with colleagues about my experiences both in the classroom with teachers and with children, I am often told that I communicate a real passion for children and learning. I have come to see that children are rich in resources and that they are capable of many things. It may be surprising to note that my current thinking is a radical departure from my mind-set of fifteen years ago. When I entered the field of early childhood education, I had a mind-set of "educating our most vulnerable citizens." I wanted them to learn and advance. I thought that direct instruction was necessary to the attainment of this goal.

It is surprising that I took my first teaching job out of college at Chicago Commons Child Development Program, because their philosophy of education conflicted with my own. However, as I became involved in the life of the classroom, I began to see the reciprocity in the process of education. The children began to teach me things that I thought I already knew. I began to see how their interests and questions could lead to exploration and learning. I watched other, more experienced Commons teachers plan their lessons around what the children were interested in, using children's investigations and questions. My mind-set was changed as I saw documentation and observations of children in the *process of learning*, not just memorizing facts. Consequently, my heart changed to seeing children as the capable citizens they are, not the empty vessels many mistake them for.

I have come to believe firmly that pursuing children's interest is at the heart of child-centered curriculum. I have learned that when teachers have a listening ear and an open heart, they can learn with and from children. Now I work as an education specialist at Chicago Commons, helping other teachers on their journey of being more child centered. Sometimes this requires teachers to readjust their perspective and goals, just as I had to. When this shift happens, this newfound flexibility yields immeasurable benefits for both children and adults.

While doing my student teaching as part of the masters program at Roosevelt University, I began a journey into the study of castles with a group of three- to five-year-old children at the Chicago Commons Nia Family Center. The study began with teachers observing the children building in the block area. As I observed, I noticed that the children were working as a cohesive group to build massive structures. Each child had input in the building, and the children always used every single block. I was fascinated with their ability to collaborate and share the decision-making responsibilities.

I sat with the children for about two weeks, just documenting observations through words and pictures. The teachers and I reviewed all of the documentation in our team meeting. They informed me that the children had been building houses for about two months. I continued to observe and document because I was looking for ways to support the children in their interest in houses, building, and construction. After several weeks of observation, the children began to talk with me about what they were building. Erik said, "This is a sand castle." It was the very first time that castles were mentioned by the children. After reflecting on the dialogue and photographs from the past two weeks, I began to see the possibility of castles becoming a recurring theme. I could see how the size of a large structure would lend itself to the image of a castle. I also began to see how the children could use the structure for dramatic play.

I've learned that to stay child centered, it's important to pay attention to what children already know. So, as teachers, we asked ourselves what we would like the children to gain from the experience of studying castles. After this discussion, I began to consider how I could support them in building upon their current knowledge. Paying attention to the children's real interest helps teachers better scaffold children's learning rather than taking over with a teacher agenda. Because the children's focus was in building, we decided to provide them with materials to see whether their interest in castles would grow. I researched and purchased a No Ends construction set and also castle blocks. The No Ends construction set allowed the children to make different shapes, such as arches and circles. I bought castle blocks because I wanted them to have hands-on reference materials that showed the structure of the castles.

During the months that followed our initial study of castles, the children began to focus on other experiences in the classroom. And I began to notice that they seemed less enthusiastic about building. I was unsure whether they had completely shifted their focus or whether they just needed a fresh perspective to rekindle their interest. I wanted to provide them with a new challenge in relation to castles to determine whether they were still interested.

I began searching our environment for ideas and resources that we could use to research whether the children would renew their interest in castles. I found a book titled *Peoples and Places of the Past* (1983). This book has a whole section on castles and cathedrals and provided us with an opportunity to connect children's knowledge to some of the academic areas that we wanted them to be successful in. For instance, we had a discussion about where castles are in the world (geography), what castles were used for (history), and who lived in the castles (anthropology). I also introduced concepts of a castle's architecture as well as new vocabulary words, such as "tower," "bridge," "drawbridge," and "moat." Our discussion went on for more than forty-five minutes. I asked the children whether they would like to draw a picture of a castle, and several were eager to participate. This showed me that children do have a long attention span when teachers focus on things children care about. They always surprise me when I watch their hearts meet up with their minds. The children went through the book and chose pictures to use as models for drawing. Interestingly, each child focused on a different aspect: towers, arches, windows, and people who live in castles. When children completed their castle drawings, we discussed each one.

Rochelle: I made a castle.

Deterrio: My castle big and big and bigger.

Erik: The castle has all the windows and the moat. The moat is dirty, and the dragon is hot. The fire make it hot. Too many castle. I made for the princess and the knights.

Cassius: This is the castle with them knights and the dark lights. It be dark in there. The kings pull out the sword and put it on the knights. Then they die!

Endrick: (no comment)

After this introduction to different castles, we embarked on a journey of research and discovery. The children used other books, photos, the Internet, and their imaginations to draw and construct castles. In particular Endrick, the child who made no comment about his castle drawing, began to show a deep interest in castles. While the other children began to find other interests in the classroom, Endrick's interest only increased. He continued to draw and construct castles. He even had a "Castle Folder" that he used to collect all his drawings and photos. After many months of exploring castles, I felt that we had exhausted all the possibilities for research and study. I asked the children to help us decide where to go next. Endrick suggested that we build a castle for the playground.

As teachers, we had to ask ourselves how to construct the experience so that the children would be successful in meeting this goal. Turning to children for curriculum ideas can introduce a fresh perspective on a focus that appears to be stagnating. We decided that Endrick's idea would be the final step in our study of castles. However, we needed to introduce some little steps in between before we could get to the finish line.

I took the photo of the castle that Endrick chose and met with my colleague Jesus Oviedo, our program studio coordinator. He was familiar with the castle study because we talked about it often in our weekly coordinator meetings. At Commons, coordinators meet weekly to discuss what classrooms are focusing on so that we know how to assist and support them. We've discovered this dialogue is essential to child-centered curriculum because time must be devoted to reviewing documentation, reflecting on experiences, and brainstorming where to go next. Jesus suggested that we meet with Endrick to discuss a variety of options to bring to life his idea of building a castle on the playground.

We decided to build a model and brainstormed some ideas on materials that would be easy for the children to manipulate. After considering a variety of options, Jesus recommended that we use Styrofoam. This material would be strong, lightweight, and easy to cut and manipulate. Jesus then purchased a variety of Styrofoam pieces and shapes from our local art supply store. In May, five months after the interest in castles emerged, we began constructing our model for the playground castle that Endrick suggested. We encouraged Endrick to take the lead in beginning the Styrofoam construction.

After the model Styrofoam castle was completed, we began preparing to build the castle for the playground. As adults, we felt at times that the project would never come to fruition. Nevertheless, we wanted to follow through with helping the children realize their dream of building a large castle for the playground. We decided to use wood because of its durability and ease of manipulation. In addition, we wanted to be environmentally responsible. We purchased large quantities of scrap pieces and plywood. It took another six months, but the castle for the playground was finally completed.

Throughout the study, the children were the main protagonists. The teachers and coordinators used observation, reflection, and provocation to dig deeper and uncover new knowledge and understanding. For instance, as we read our observations and studied the children's words and drawings and our photographs, we looked for connections between ideas, experiences, and the construction of tangible objects. The children were encouraged to dream, plan, draw, and construct castles. We had many meetings and much discussion. However, the children drove the study.

As we look back on this study, we have many thoughts to keep us learning. We wonder: "What is it about castles that held such deep interest for low-income Head Start children in a large urban city in America?" "What influenced their ideas when many of them had never seen a real castle?" One child in particular, Endrick, made the study a part of our everyday lives. We learned to keep our focus on the children's interests and our shared goal. As a result, this experience was not about learning outcomes (although there were many), it was about supporting the ideas and deep interests of the children. Our belief that children are deep thinkers and competent beyond our initial expectations was a strong presence throughout the many months of study. The teachers and the children bonded as we all learned more.

► Share Your Reflections with Kristie

Write a letter to Kristie at KristieNorwood29@gmail.com with your reflections on how she discovered that the power of observation enhanced her child-centered curriculum approach. Consider including your thoughts about the following:

- What influenced Kristie to change her view of education from direct instruction to following children's interests?
- What role did studying observations and documentation with colleagues play in Kristie's work to follow the children's lead?
- How did Kristie's work with the children on the castle project meet learning outcomes for the children?

► *Practice What You've Learned*

Notes about Your Current Observation Practices

Use the questions on this page to help you reflect on your current observation practices.

How would you assess your current observation and documentation skills?

_____

_____

_____

_____

_____

What are the barriers that keep you from regular observation?

_____

_____

_____

_____

_____

_____

_____

_____

What strategies could you use to overcome these barriers?

_____

_____

_____

_____

_____

_____

_____

_____

How do you use your observations in your curriculum planning?

_____

_____

_____

_____

_____

_____

_____

_____

Redefining Curriculum Themes

 Beginning Reflections

As you observe children at play, what themes in their actions and conversations do they return to over and over again?

_____

_____

_____

_____

When you plan curriculum, how much do you focus on offering experiences related to these themes?

_____

_____

_____

_____

_____

Redefining theme planning is an important part of adopting a child-centered emergent curriculum approach.

Because the weather warmed up, Amanda decided to take the sensory table outside for her group of three-year-olds. That first day, she took out a large plastic tub filled with birdseed and a variety of baskets and containers. Almost immediately, the children began filling and pouring the seeds into the containers and baskets. Then one child carried a full basket across the play yard, calling "Birdie, Birdie, here's your food." Soon the entire group was filling containers and spreading birdseed throughout the yard.

The next week, Amanda filled the sensory table with water and added containers, spouts, and buckets. Again, the children initially played at the table, but before long, their activity turned to carrying the water across the yard. Noticing this transportation theme, Amanda brought out toy trucks, buses, and wagons. Then she added lunch boxes, baskets with handles, bags, and other boxes. All month, the children's play centered on loading, carrying, wheeling, pushing, and unloading things across the yard. Amanda began to notice opportunities to introduce concepts from the physical sciences—mechanics and motion, simple and complex movement, the physics of motion—and introduced related vocabulary through her conversations with the children and descriptions of what she saw them doing.

Most preschool curriculum is planned around themes. Whether they are important outcomes for children or not, topical themes become the focus of bulletin boards, group times, and art activities throughout the week. But does this theme planning have a pertinent context for the children? Does it reflect their real lives or interests? How do topical themes such as holidays, dinosaurs, colors, or letters of the week relate to early learning standards? Meaningful outcomes for children can only happen with intentional thinking on the part of the teacher. They do not occur when teachers habitually reach into their box of favorite activities.

Transportation is a common theme in preschool curriculums. Typically, a teacher will include art activities, fingerplays, dramatic play, and field trips to help children learn about trucks, boats, trains, and planes. Teachers search curriculum "recipe books" for ideas and activities, never stopping to consider what the children's interest or current understandings are about the theme.

In the previous story, Amanda came to the theme of transportation following a very different route. She used her observation skills to discover the children's theme of transportation. Amanda also used the children's clear interest in transporting the birdseed to introduce concepts and language related to the learning domain of science. She understands that complex learning can occur when she supports and extends these meaningful child-initiated activities.

Redefining theme planning—by observing children and using their interests to focus on and extend the learning—is an important part of adopting a child-centered emergent curriculum approach.

From Topical Themes to Developmental Themes

Looking at something from a child's perspective can help you redefine the entire concept of themes. Given the opportunity, children will pursue tasks and skills that are optimal for their individual developmental level. If you watch closely, children will often surprise you with their knowledge and competency. As skilled observers of children, teachers can discover the deeper meaning, or developmental themes, children are engaged in and use these themes for curriculum planning. Teachers can also study how children's interests naturally lead to explorations of learning domains such as literacy, math, and science. This mind-set and teaching approach can fuel projects or investigations that engage the minds of both children and teachers.

Traditional Theme Planning	Developmental Theme Planning
The teacher picks a weekly theme and plans a variety of activities to cover information related to the topic.	The teacher observes children to uncover the deeper meaning, developmental themes, or learning domains reflected in the children's play. The teacher provides further materials and activities to sustain significant pursuits.
The teacher designs activities to provide information and uses questions and work sheets to teach and "test" for correct answers.	The teacher bases her approach on exploring the children's questions, remembering their real lives and relationships, and striving to understand what draws them to this play or exploration.
The teacher places emphasis on "naming to know" and reciting information that the children are "supposed" to learn.	The teacher plans materials and activities to provoke curiosity and uncover what the children already know. The teacher also looks for possible misunderstandings and ways for the children to reexamine their understandings or conclusions.
The teacher assesses children's missing skills and knowledge in order to plan what to teach them.	The teacher places emphasis on "doing to know"—interaction and investigation with materials, people, and ideas interesting to the children, while connecting with concepts and language related to learning domains.
The teacher bases the teaching approach on a narrow, simplistic view of learning and school readiness, focusing only on basic skills and superficial understandings.	The teacher's planning revolves around the children's strengths and interests. Discovering ways to integrate early learning standards with children's existing questions and ideas is central to the process.

Children's Play Themes

The pages that follow include a variety of ways to identify children's developmental themes. These themes can be used to create a child-centered emergent curriculum. You can launch these from your general knowledge of children's interests in response to observations you have been making or in response to something unfolding in the greater community. Remember to keep analyzing the possible deeper meaning of children's themes and the connection to learning domains as you observe children's ongoing play and conversations. Based on your observations and reflections, provide additional materials and activities to extend their interest.

Piaget identified four stages of children's play that are useful for planning and responding to children in relevant ways:

- exploration
- construction play
- pretend play
- playing games with rules

When you closely observe children, you will see these developmental themes underlying their approach to play. The following stories offer an example of each stage of play and show several ways to provide materials and activities to enhance each play theme.

Exploration

Frankie is playing in the housekeeping area. He stands in front of the play refrigerator opening and closing the door over and over again. He seems to have no interest in what is on the shelves. Instead, Frankie is listening intently to the squeaking sound the door makes as he closes it.

Children use their senses to try things out, to find out how things work, and to learn cause and effect. You can help them enhance their play by asking questions that explore the developmental perspectives of a child, such as the following:

- How does this feel, sound, taste, smell, move?
- What parts and properties does this have?
- How is this like something I already know? How is it different?
- What can I make this thing do?

Provide for Exploration

Once a theme emerges in children's play, plan activities and interactions to sustain and enrich learning. Keep in mind the distinction between topical themes and developmental themes or tasks children are pursuing to grow into their competency. One idea is to make collections of things available to the children. For instance, a collection of loose parts is a great way to provision the environment for each of Piaget's stages of play.

Let the children explore the following collections on their own, use the collections in combination with each other, or offer them to a child to enhance the pursuit of an interest or idea. Sensory materials and loose parts are the best for children who are involved in exploratory play. Here are some examples:

Tubes and Cylinders. PVC pipe, toilet paper and paper towel rolls, kaleidoscopes, clear plastic tubing of different lengths and thicknesses.

Balls. Ping-Pong balls, Wiffle balls, golf balls, rubber balls, Nerf balls, racquetballs, baseballs, beach balls, tennis balls, softballs, cotton balls, teething balls, Styrofoam balls, string balls, yarn balls, pom-poms.

Letting the children put the balls, tubes, and cylinders together will prompt exploration of fitting balls in tubes, watching them roll through, and filling tubes with balls.

Things That Tickle and Jingle. Feathers, soft brushes, fur, wigs, scarves, silk, feather duster, tinsel; cow bell, jingle bell, clog bell, wrist bells, ankle bells, school bell, brass bell, wind chimes.

Things to See Through. Eyeglasses, sunglasses, goggles, binoculars, telescope, camera lens, Plexiglas, Mylar, plastic bottle, theater gel, colored cellophane, magnifying glass, microscope, jeweler's loupe.

Sensory Materials. Mud, soil, clay, wet sand, white sand, black sand, sand with glitter, ice cubes, ice blocks, crushed ice, snow, shaving cream, soap suds, bubbles, water balloons, straw or hay, freshly mowed grass, gravel, wood shavings, shredded paper, confetti, shells, rocks, seeds (pumpkin, sunflower, grass), birdseed, pinecones, fall leaves, moss, flower petals, evergreen needles and boughs, twigs, eggs, eggshells, worms in soil, bean sprouts in soil, spun wool, buttons, felt pieces, cotton balls, leather scraps.

Put these materials in a tub or sensory table, alone or in combination with scoops, funnels, and tubes, and watch children become engaged in deep exploration and sensory joy.

Construction Play

Jason carefully searches through the bucket of blocks for the long rectangle. He begins building by attaching a set of wheels to a base. He adds a set of doors and a roof. As he puts short, square pieces on the top, he says, "I'm making a car."

Children move from sensory exploration to having a definite plan for exploration. Think about how a child would answer these questions:

- How can I combine these different things?
- What can I build with these?
- Can I make this look like something I know?

Provide for Construction Play

Along with the many toys geared toward building and construction, try adding unusual collections of open-ended materials to encourage construction. Add a variety of ways to connect things to other things.

Tape. Duct tape, masking tape, electrical tape, cellophane tape, packing tape, colored cloth tape of different widths and colors, gaffer tape, sticky dots and squares, file folder labels, stickers of all kinds.

Tools. Hole punch, leather punch, stapler, glue gun, sewing machine, hammer, screwdriver, pliers, wrench.

Connectors. Toothpicks, playdough, Styrofoam, straw, yarn, string, clothespins, wire, nails, twist ties, paper clips, thumbtacks, rubber bands, brad fasteners, clips, rings, diaper pins.

Pretend Role Plays

Diego runs up to the top of the short hill. He drags a long rope behind him. He pretends to have a hard time pulling the rope. "Come on, you big cow!" he says, as he grunts and pulls.

You will often see children move and add to their construction play by acting out ideas and feelings using numerous props. They are intuitively exploring questions like the following:

•   What can I make this thing be?

•   How can I use this for my role play?

•   What can these other things and people become in my play?

Typical dress-up clothes, pretend housekeeping equipment, and a variety of traditional prop boxes (such as gas station, store, restaurant, hospital, firefighter, and office props) are all important materials for pretend role play. A number of common social and emotional themes also arise during pretend play. Here are some ideas that will enhance these themes.

Birthdays

Children often talk about birthdays, birthday parties, cakes, and candles. These celebrations provide a special ritual and sense of importance and power in childhood. Children use birthday parties as a bargaining chip in negotiating relationships. They will frequently say to one another, "If you let me play, you can be my best friend and come to my birthday."

To build on this popular theme, create a prop box with calendars, growth charts with photos, candles, decorations, cake pans, playdough for the cakes, party favors, hats, boxes, wrapping paper, bows, tape, and materials to make invitations and thank-you notes.

As children play, listen to the fascinating ideas and understandings they pursue about friendship, the passage of time, aging, and celebration. These are the deeper themes of significance in this birthday play.

Separation

Separation anxiety is common among young children. Moving away from family into the larger world of preschool and child care is a difficult transition for many children.

Through dramatic play and story time, children can act out their fears and gain understanding and power over separation issues. Make up your own stories using small dramatic play characters and puppets or felt pieces as props. Then leave these out for the children to play with.

Reading books to children and then creating prop boxes or felt pieces related to the stories about separation provide opportunities for children to "play" with these powerful issues. Some good books about separation include the following:

- *Are You My Mother?* by P. D. Eastman
- *The Leaving Morning* by Angela Johnson

- *Mama, Do You Love Me?* by Barbara M. Joosse

- *Mommy, Don't Go* by Elizabeth Crary

- *Oh My Baby, Little One* by Kathi Appelt

- *The Runaway Bunny* by Margaret Wise Brown

- *Will You Come Back for Me?* by Ann Tompert

Children's Fears

Observe children's activities and interactions for themes related to their fears and insecurities. Some children are afraid of monsters or the dark. For many children, hurricanes, earthquakes, floods, and fires are part of an annual cycle. Others experience violence, murder, and stories of gangs and war. Increasingly, children have firsthand experience with life-threatening situations or a death in the family.

Children feel helpless and powerless to take care of themselves in the world. The strong popularity of superheroes in the media reflects children's need to act out powerful, invincible roles. Rather than forbidding superhero play or avoiding scary issues, respond and create curriculum around them. Here are some examples of teacher efforts using children's fears and emotions to engage them in real learning.

Floods

Barb's child care program is next to a river that had its one-hundred-year flood while she and the children watched. For weeks the children observed helicopters landing with sandbags and volunteers fighting to keep the river back.

The children's play reflected what they were seeing each day. They used books and blocks to build a dike and took turns pretending to be the river that broke through. Barb added helicopters, small people figures, and picture books about rivers and floods. She transferred these props to the water table and added some sand. Floods became the topical theme of the children's play for weeks. Underneath this topic was the developmental theme of getting control over their fears.

Earthquakes

After an earthquake shook her community, Sharon and her children took turns building a town with blocks and props on top of a wobbly table. Each time their town was built, they shook the table and watched as the earthquake toppled the buildings. They built and knocked down their town over and over again. Sharon added props to let the children act out the powerful roles of medics, firefighters, and construction workers.

Power Stories

Watching superhero play all week in his class, Tom approached a small group of children with a pen and a homemade blank book he keeps for these occasions. He sat near the play and asked the children to tell him their power stories.

As the children talked, he wrote down what they said. "I'm the strongest one in the world," said Anthony. "I can even pick up houses. Laser beams come out of my eyes and turn people to stone and ice. Then they go to sleep forever." The other children joined in, adding their ideas to the power story.

Soon the aggressive play had changed to an engaged, meaningful discussion. The children cooperatively designed costumes and props to build on their story themes.

Tom read the power stories later during circle time. He noticed that other children were as engrossed in the stories as those who created them. He sought out his coworkers for more ideas on how to work with the power theme.

Games

Jessica and Ryan balance long blocks vertically in one corner of the block area. From the other side they roll cylinder-shaped blocks toward these long blocks. As blocks are knocked down, they remind each other of the score and whose turn is next.

Piaget says that when children are in this stage of play, they agree on a set of rules to follow for a game. As they play with materials, they are considering these possible questions:

- Can I play a game with these?
- What rules are needed for this game?
- How can we make this game more fun?

Provide for Games

In addition to commercial games (which should be evaluated to ensure that they are nonbiased, inclusive, gender fair, and promote coopera-tion), stock the classroom with a supply of props for child-created games. Watch for opportunities to offer these props to children when they seem engaged in a game play theme.

Game Props

Here are some suggestions for game props:

- ball, cylinder, beanbag, large cardboard for designing and making a variety of game boards with props
- spinner, dice, coin for taking turns

- watch, clock, and timer for taking turns

- chart paper, clipboard, and paper and pens for making lists and keeping score

- pictures, photographs, blank cards, boxes, and cardboard for game boards that can be created and played with over and over

Meaningful Work Themes

Children love to be involved with real work. They want to help carry, fix, cook, build, wash, plan, and organize things. Children develop a strong identity and a sense of both independence and interdependence when they participate in activities that contribute to their family and classroom community. Providing for this kind of involvement is a critical component of a child-centered curriculum.

Cleanup Kits

Let children do real cleaning, vacuuming, and washing. Provide readily accessible, safe, and nontoxic materials and encouragement for children to participate. They love to help clean up and sweep the floor using child-sized brooms and dustpans, handheld vacuums, and vacuum cleaners.

Provide spray bottles filled with a vinegar and water solution and sponges for cleaning tables; window cleaner, squeegees, and paper towels for washing windows and tubs; and buckets, sponges, soap, and dish towels for washing dishes, tables, furniture, and toys.

Mealtime Preparation and Setup

Setting the table, serving food, and cleaning up afterward are all valuable tasks. Rather than just an occasional cooking project, plan and provide regular ways for children to help select and prepare food. This cultivates an identity for children as being responsible members of a community. In addition they acquire a variety of desirable skills, including planning, social conversation and negotiation, one-to-one correspondence, counting, and knowledge about health and nutrition.

Naptime Setup and Cleanup

The transition in and out of naptime will be smoother and less of an imposition on children when they are put in charge of getting things set out and put away. Help children learn the scope and sequence of the tasks involved, perhaps by making a step-by-step chart for the children to illustrate and refer to. You may even involve children in developing a map of where the nap cots go and have them use this as another reference tool.

Classroom Maintenance, Repair, and Replacements

Put together a tool kit so children can help tape ripped books and bindings or fix an appliance or toy. As materials need replacing, have children participate in selecting and ordering things to be purchased. Together read the instructions and make a plan for regular maintenance. Engaging in caring for and repairing materials reminds children to be stewards, rather than consumers of resources. In the process, they develop important small-motor skills and acquire knowledge about assembling, construction, and mechanical functions.

Lesson Planning and Recording

Have children participate in planning, preparing, and documenting your curriculum. Conduct discussions with them about who is learning what. Involve them in collecting samples of their work and dictated words. Collect photos of what has been happening in the classroom and display them. Involve the children in selecting things for their individual portfolios.

Helping Their Classmates

As much as possible, refer children to each other for help. They can assist each other in learning how to zip, tie, and use a toy or a tool. Children can offer comfort and help to someone in need. Rather than just a jobs chart, a classroom helper's chart could be a skills bank or a resource map for regular referral.

Physical Development Themes

Unlike adults, who can pretend that their bodies are inconsequential to the process of using their brains, children bring their bodies with them wherever they go. Teachers often remind children to use "inside voices" or "walking feet," and to sit "crisscross applesauce." Do you tend to treat outdoor play as a time to burn off steam rather than a way to build bodies? Many female teachers, socialized to have their bodies seen and not developed, often neglect children's physical development themes.

Most children are kinesthetic learners and need to move around as a way of paying attention and learning. For these and all other children, provide for active bodies in your classroom—don't just tolerate them.

Body Themes

Simple materials and equipment—offered daily both indoors and outdoors—encourage the kind of physical movement that is so important
for children's physical, cognitive, and social development. If creeping
and crawling is the curriculum theme for the day, then the materials
and activities you offer should provide for these skills. For example, you
might set up obstacle courses, making tunnels with blankets and tables
and creating passageways with large boxes.

Props for Active Bodies

Here are some more ideas for materials and activities to enhance and challenge moving bodies:

- pillows and mattresses to build with, hide under, jump on, or rest on

- wagons, carts, buckets, boxes, and heavy things to lift and move

- balls, beanbags, balloons, and bubbles to chase, reach and jump for, pound, pop, and swing at

- steps, ladders, trees, wooden planks, sheets, blankets, and large spools to build ever-changing and challenging places to climb, jump, and hide

- mirrors to see yourself and your body moving

- shovels, ropes, and pulleys for building and inventing

- riding toys, bikes, trikes, roller skates, and push-and-pull toys for negotiating speed, balance, and terrain and for transporting materials and people from place to place

- milk cartons, cardboard tubes, and inflated inner tubes, rope, and other loose parts to build and invent with

- large mounds or hills of dirt, grass and sand, grassy fields, bushes, trees, water, holes, tunnels, and hiding places to experience the sensory joys and the physical challenges that only nature can provide

Now it's your turn to practice. Here are more body movements you might see children exploring. Look over the list, and in the space provided brainstorm possible materials and activities you could offer.

Movements You See

Materials and Activities to Offer

pushing
pulling
scooting

running
dancing
marching
chasing

retrieving
carrying
loading
unloading
lifting
digging
hiding

pounding
knocking down
throwing
picking up
balancing

bouncing
jumping
kicking
pedaling
swinging

Creative Expression Themes

Traditional early childhood creative expression curriculum (including arts and crafts, music, and block building) usually involves a product. Teachers plan projects for children to make, or ask questions about what the children are *making*, rather than what they are *doing*. Typical questions include, "What color is that?" "Can you count how many you made?" Though teachers typically say, "The process is more important than the product," what they give attention to and post on the walls are

the products. Traditionally excluded is any description of the process that engaged the children in creating these products. When you look at the process children go through during these creative activities, you will discover developmental stages that are usually more important than a final product.

Stages of Creative Expression

Exploring. As in other play arenas, children begin creative expression activities by exploring the properties of materials. They examine, manipulate, experiment, and repeatedly try things. This exploration is an important step in learning to use materials for representing ideas and feelings. It leads to using materials as thinking tools in future explorations.

Exploring behavior leading to creative expression can look something like the following:

- Block building: knocking down structures created by others; carrying blocks around and putting them down in specific places; experimenting with connecting and stacking blocks

- Painting: smearing and exploring paint; using hands to paint with; painting one's body; dabbing with a brush; painting lines similar to scribbles; covering whole areas of the paper with paint

- Using playdough: manipulating and transforming dough to represent their ideas; pinching, squeezing, and pounding dough or clay; rolling it to make coils and balls

Naming. As children explore and use materials, they begin to notice something they want to name. You've probably seen examples like these:

- Block building: As Tamara continues stacking and connecting, she says, "I made a house."

- Painting: When Jasmine uses big arm movements to smear the green paint back and forth across the paper, she exclaims, "I'm making a tree."

- Using playdough: Making balls, coils, and other forms, Jamal talks of snakes, pancakes, cars, and birthday cakes.

Representing. As children learn to explore and use tools, they intentionally begin to create representations. Their representations include props for pretending and role-playing, along with design and building creations. Unlike teacher-planned arts and crafts, which represent adult views, children's creative products represent their own thinking and learning, often revealing complexity and personal or social significance.

Consider the skills and ideas these children express:

- Block building: Taiko has a small hamster at home. Today at preschool, she announces her plans to build a house for the hamster in the block area. She finds the block shapes she wants to use and builds an initial structure with long corridors and small covelike areas. She says, "This is for my hamster to run through. And these places are for food so he can stop to eat whenever he gets hungry." She goes searching for more shapes to add to her already complex piece of architecture.

- Drawing and painting: Gabrielle spends the whole morning at the art table making pictures of her family. She adds more color and detail to each one and includes a slightly different emphasis to distinguish them. She says to her friend, "Here we are eating dinner," and "Here's a picture of me and my mom in our backyard. See, my mom, Jacquie, just cut the grass so it doesn't hide the mosquitoes."

- Using playdough: Sam and Jacob are working with the playdough and a set of plastic dishes and pans. They are cooking dinner using the playdough as the food. "Let's have hamburgers for our dinner," says Sam. "Okay," answers Jacob. "I'll make the burgers and you make the buns." They work together and create an elaborate representation with the playdough, including blobs for the ketchup and snake shapes for the French fries.

Provide for Creative Expression

To make life easy, are you limiting paint to only two or three color choices at the easel? Do you stop the children from mixing the paint and the paintbrushes? Do you offer only predesigned art projects for children to copy?

When you provide opportunities for experiencing the *processes* of creative expression rather than having the goal of a product, you address developmental themes that are engaging children. Set up your art and sensory areas to include an array of open-ended materials to combine and transform. Plan for and allow the variety of approaches and uses that each child will bring to the creative process.

When teachers focus on processes rather than products, they help children learn more about the possibilities in the materials and allow children to express their personal developmental themes. Children learn to use materials as "thinking tools," not merely products to consume or create.

Painting Activities

Think of painting as a process for exploration rather than as an end product. Plan and provide ways for children to experiment with painting by offering a variety of paper and other objects to paint on, an array of implements to paint with, and different substances to use as paint.

Choose materials from the following lists to have available in your art area. Offer a wide variety of choices, not just one or two.

Paper to Use

- adding machine tape, envelopes
- bags and boxes of all sizes and shapes
- cardboard, butcher paper, newsprint
- wrapping paper, wallpaper, greeting cards
- coffee filters, foil, waxed paper, sandpaper, Styrofoam
- folders, index cards, junk mail, computer paper, construction paper

Substances to Paint With

- tempera paint, watercolor, fingerpaint, food coloring
- glass wax, liquid starch, condensed milk, salt, flour
- mud, soap flakes, shaving cream

- glue (white and colored)
- water
- textures to add to paint: sugar, sand, cornmeal, glitter, extracts

Objects to Paint With

- brushes of all kinds: scrub brush, vegetable brush, bottle brush, toothbrush, hairbrush, paintbrush, barbecue grill brush, makeup brush, whisk broom, feather duster, nail brush
- kitchen items of all kinds: potato masher, baster, cookie cutter, sponge, scouring pad, chopsticks, berry basket, egg carton, jar lid, fly swatter, straw, rolling pin, cork, candle, toothpick
- items from nature: pinecone, leaf, evergreen bough, flower, corncob, rock, shell, feather, sunflower, twig, branch
- miscellaneous items: sponge brushes and rollers of all sizes, string, yarn, rope, toy car, eyedropper, squeeze bottle, spray bottle, marbles, plastic golf balls, spool, carpet piece, cotton, spun wool

Objects to Paint On

- paper, box, linoleum, fabric
- rock, shell
- wood, twig, branch, brick, tile
- glass, mirror, metal can, bottle
- bag, plate, basket, tray, pan
- body, hand, foot, face

Transformation Activities

Children are fascinated by activities and materials they can manipulate, change, and transform. Children use their senses to learn about the world, so they are drawn to activities that involve all the senses. Through these transformational activities, children observe, make predictions, and develop problem-solving skills. They learn about the world of science, physics, chemistry, and mathematics in appropriate, hands-on ways. Stretch your comfort level with messiness and plan for these engaging activities with children.

Magical Potions

Expand beyond a traditional water table and sandbox. Provide children with exciting materials that change and grow as the children mix and shake. Add pitchers, containers, and utensils to tubs or the sensory table, mix in the following materials, and then sit back and watch children make discoveries:

- Flour and water get sticky and gooey like glue.

- Flour dough with yeast rises, grows, and smells terrific.

- Vinegar and baking soda smoke and fizzle.

- Warm milk, food coloring, and dish soap magically swirl together.

- Cornstarch and water become a goopy substance that stays firm when you squeeze it but drips when you open your hand.

- Glue, water, and borax mixed together become a blubbery substance that stretches when you hold it and makes bubbles when you blow it.

- Blocks of ice laced with food coloring transform to colorful ice caves when rock salt is poured on top.

- Plain dirt and water create that ever-so-delightful substance—mud!

Life Cycle Observations

The natural change of the seasons and all of the living things of the world are wonderful transformation processes to observe together. Provide opportunities to observe life cycles throughout your curriculum. Go hunting for them in your yard or neighborhood.

- Hatch baby chicks from eggs.

- Compost food to use as fertilizer for a garden.

- Grow a garden together and watch things go from seed to flower to fruit and back to the compost bin.

- Observe and document someone's pregnancy.

- Document the children's own life cycle using photos from home (from infancy to the present) and design charts for measuring children's growth in height and weight.

- Watch caterpillars spin their cocoons and hatch into butterflies.

- Create a special ritual observing and documenting the changing seasons: keep track of the light and dark together, measure the temperature changes and the differences in people's clothing and daily lives, and collect items from nature that reflect the changes.

Learning Skills

As children become interested in representing their ideas and experiences, they need more skills to accomplish their plans. They may seek help in using tools to make what they have in mind.

Many teachers are uncertain of their role in teaching skills to young children. Some try to do so before children show interest or have a meaningful context for learning the skill. This usually causes frustration and feelings of failure. Other teachers avoid teaching skills, thinking a child-centered approach means no direct instruction. If children have no skills to carry out their ideas, this can also result in frustration and failure.

When children are ready to learn, they need to serve as an apprentice with a mentor or coach. Helpful instructions, demonstrations, and breaking down tasks for skill building are appropriate teacher interventions. Stay alert to cues that children are ready for some help. These are teachable moments.

As you read the following examples of children's work, think about how you might respond to them:

- Robert has used playdough to make all of the parts of a dog: a body, four legs, and a head. He is having trouble firmly connecting the parts so the dog will stand up. He asks Miss Williams, "Will you fix my dog for me?"

- Rebecca tells the teacher, "I want to paint a picture of a butterfly. Will you help me?"

- Masayo is making a tall tower with the blocks. She has been working to connect two towers with a bridge. Each time she tries, the towers fall over. Masayo looks at her teacher and asks, "Can you make it work?"

One of the golden rules of early childhood education is to encourage children to do things for themselves. The underlying goal of this rule is to help children feel capable and proud of what they can do on their own. Teachers have been warned to avoid providing models for children to copy so that children will not compare their lesser efforts to those of adults. However, in the above examples, a teacher following these rules would miss the developmental opportunities in these children's requests.

Robert needs help to accomplish his goal of putting the dog together. He has thought through his ideas and come up with a representation himself. Rather than leaving him discouraged, the teacher can offer support by asking questions, making suggestions, and giving a helping hand if needed. For example, you could demonstrate how to attach one of the body parts and let him finish the rest.

Rebecca may know what butterflies look like and even have an idea about one she would like to paint. The teacher can assess her efforts and help Rebecca explore her ideas with probing questions and suggestions. Rebecca might also benefit from looking through picture books and magazines with photographs of butterflies and butterfly paintings to help her formulate her representation. The teacher could offer a demonstration of how to use paint so Rebecca can get the results she is after.

Masayo also would fare better with some questions and suggestions for analyzing what is happening as she builds so she has an understanding of where the problem is. This might prompt her to try other approaches.

In each scenario, the teacher can help by carefully observing and analyzing what the child is trying to achieve. Lev Vygotsky suggests that teacher actions can serve as a scaffold to assist children in reaching a competency just out of reach.

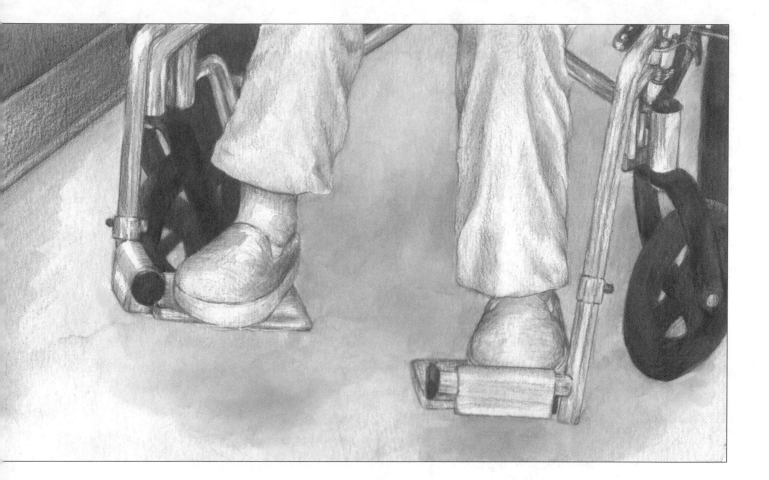

An Inspirational Story

As you read the story of Ann Pelo, notice how seriously she takes the children's ideas. Where another teacher might have passed off the ideas as unrealistic or not worth pursuing, Ann embraces them. She enriches her environment, involves the children's families, and searches for more resources. In her postscript, written a decade later, Ann describes how this project was a turning point in her professional career and, with her growth, how she might have made different decisions if this project were unfolding today.

Our School Is Not Fair:
A Story about Emergent Curriculum

Ann Pelo, Early Childhood Teacher

Early one fall, after several days of fierce debate about the differences between steam shovels and excavators, my class of nine four-year-olds visited the library, hoping to find answers to our questions. On our way back to our child care center, arms full of books about construction, we passed a church with a wheelchair accessible parking sign at the curb. One of the children asked why the sign was there and what it meant. To answer her questions, we examined the church, found a matching sign on the only door without stairs, and concluded that the door with the wheelchair sign was especially for people with wheelchairs who are not able to use stairs. The parking sign, the children figured out, saved a parking place for people who need to use the door without stairs.

In our discussion about the church and its signs, a child commented that our school (which is housed upstairs in another church building) was unfair because "We have too many stairs." Another child, Sophie, told us about her stepfather, who uses a wheelchair and who is unable to come into our school to pick her up or visit her. She told us that they have a ramp at their house for him to use. Several children exclaimed, "We need to build a ramp at our school!"

There on the sidewalk, late for lunch, arms heavy with books, faces sure and excited, the children challenged me to listen attentively and throw in my hat with them. "This is for serious," one of the children stated, and I was with them—we would try to build a ramp at our school.

During the walk back to school and through lunch, we created a list of what we might need to build a ramp. I encouraged the children to think of steps we would need to take before we could plunge into the actual building. And then it was naptime. I caught my breath and reviewed what had happened. I was embarking on a journey with the children. My responsibilities during this journey involved careful balancing of two seemingly contrary tasks: (1) attentive listening to the children; watching them for cues about their interests, skills, questions, and knowledge; and responding to what I heard and saw; and (2) introducing ideas, initiating exploration, and leading the children into new territory. These are the challenges of emergent curriculum for me: responding and anticipating, following and initiating.

During naptime on that first day, I wrote a note to the parents in my class, explaining what we'd embarked on. I began talking with my coworkers, my director, and our center's trainer, alerting people to this emerging curriculum focus on accessibility. I asked for resources, thoughts, and support.

I also sketched a curriculum web with "wheelchair accessibility/ramp building" in the center. This made tangible the challenge of following while leading. This initial web, I knew, must not become "the curriculum plan for the month" if our accessibility project was to remain responsive to the children's discoveries, questions, and passions. Instead, this web would serve as a way to focus my thinking, to generate ideas for stocking the classroom with props, and to prepare for the surprises that would come from the children and their families as we pursued this project. In my thinking about emergent curriculum, I saw this initial web more as a guidebook for traveling, with reminders to "be ready for . . . ," "be sure to spend some time at . . . ," and "bring along . . .". This web would not be a map marked in red to be followed unwaveringly.

And so I stocked the environment with building materials, seriation and classification games using nuts and bolts, ramp-shaped blocks, and books about construction and people using wheelchairs. I borrowed a wheelchair and brought in a persona doll in a wheelchair. These wheelchairs led us to accessibility issues about our classroom: Children used the chair during our daily meetings and noticed how different our meeting circle looked. They used the wheelchair during work time and found that they couldn't reach the lowest shelves in our room. They tried to use the wheelchair to go to the bathroom and discovered that they couldn't get through the door. We rearranged the room and added the bathroom doors to our building plans. Children wanted Carmella, the persona doll, to come to lunch with us, but since our lunchroom is downstairs, she had to remain upstairs in our classroom alone each day—and the children's passion for our project was strengthened.

As we began this accessibility project, I invited parents to join us by contributing resources, time, and interest. Several parents who are architects brought in architectural drawings, which were soon scattered around the room as children pored over them and began integrating them into their drawings. A family in our class who had recently remodeled their home brought in a mound of photos tracing their project step by step, and another family invited us to visit their torn-up attic as they began a rewiring project.

This effort toward parental involvement was difficult, highlighting some of the differences between the culture of Reggio Emilia and the affluent, professional, European American culture in which my child care center is situated. It was an effort to get parents to read notes, listen to stories, bring in resources, leave work to come on a trip with us, invite us to their homes, and transform their contact with school from drop-off/pickup to one of community involvement. It was an effort for me to let go of my position as the only adult in the classroom and be ready to add to or change my ideas, to truly welcome parents' involvement.

Early in our accessibility project, the children and I began a dialogue with members of the church with whom we share space. The children dictated a letter to the building committee, explaining that "our school is not fair" and that we hoped to build a ramp to make it fairer. The committee chairperson contacted me to say that the church had explored the possibility of building a ramp and a wheelchair lift several years earlier and had found the cost and remodeling effort involved to be more than they could undertake. Despite their prior decision not to go ahead with a ramp, I asked for support from the church for my class's project, advocating for the children's learning and experience with activism. I felt both sheepish in the face of their carefully researched decision and fiercely determined to move ahead with this project, championing the children's right to try. The church committee agreed to send a person to meet with our class and gave us the thumbs-up on our project.

Through all this, the children practiced using building tools, working long and hard at the workbench and mastering the use of hammers, saws, and drills. Children began using models and drawings to guide and represent their block building, extending their work with the architectural drawings. I invited an architect to visit and tour our school with us. She drew our attention to the concepts of slope and ramp length.

During these weeks, we took the wheelchair on trips through the neighborhood, often to Sophie's house, where her dad gave children rides on his wheelchair up and down the ramp at his house. We sketched his ramp and crafted models of it to use back at school in our project. On these trips through the neighborhood, children became increasingly frustrated as they encountered sidewalks without ramps and suggested, in their passion about unfairness, that we tell the people who make sidewalks that they must build ramps—and we did. The children dictated a letter that we sent to the city engineering department, which led to a dialogue with one of the pedestrian safety engineers. This course of activism was not in my initial web, but it was one of the surprises the children offered me during this project. Our correspondence led to several visits by the safety engineer, culminating many months later in a trip she organized for us to a neighborhood site where a sidewalk ramp was being poured; the children helped arrange the frames and smooth the wet cement. They called this ramp "their ramp" for the rest of the year.

Through all of this, I took many photos; made and kept copies of the children's letters to the church, city, and their parents; and tape-recorded conversations among the children and transcribed them. I wanted to create a record of our project, our classroom history, as it developed. I used the photos, letters, and tape recordings to look and listen closely to the children and plan from their concerns, passions, and understandings. The children used the documentation as a common frame of reference, and would often take out the "Ramp Book" (a photo album) and tell each other the stories of the photos and letters in it.

We did not build a ramp at our school. The church committee's early advice proved true. The cost and amount of remodeling required were more than we could manage. I still, in some ways, feel this as a failure.

"A Reggio school would have built the ramp," I say to myself, though I understand the many differences between my school and the Reggio schools.

The successes of this project, though, were manifold. I learned much about the challenges and value of making space and time for learning to unfold, and I began my work toward genuinely inviting parents into the life of the classroom. This four-month project assured me that listening to the children is my best guide for curriculum planning. What began as a debate about construction machinery became a passionate effort to remedy unfairness. It was sustained by the children's passion, excitement, and investment in making our school fair and by careful listening and planning that honored their passion and interests.

The children reminded me through the year of the power this project had in their lives: each building they made with blocks, each house they drew, had a ramp carefully designed for accessibility. On each field trip we took, the children noted the wheelchair-accessible parking places, becoming indignant and angry when someone parked inappropriately. And I continue to hear from their kindergarten teachers and their families about these children's awareness of fairness issues, particularly accessibility issues, and about their surety that they ought to act for fairness.

2010 Postscript: Looking Back, Looking Forward

Revisiting this story more than a decade later, I'm aware that this yearlong exploration of building a ramp set my course as a teacher. It was, for me, the coming together of my commitment to social justice teaching and my pull toward Reggio-inspired emergent teaching. In my work since that ramp project, I've braided those two threads together to form the core of my teaching practice.

During the ramp work, I gathered notes, photos, and traces of the children's work into a book that told the story of our exploration. That experience gave me a taste of the power of documentation. And over the years, documentation has become the central practice in my teaching—not simply a way to tell the stories of classroom life, but the way I plan curriculum.

With the ramp project, I experienced responsive emergent curriculum at its most exhilarating, planning step by step, moment by moment, experience by experience. The notes that I took of children's conversations, the photos and other traces of their work, guided my decisions about what materials and experiences to offer to the children. Since this project, the notion of documentation as the thinking process that supports emergent curriculum has been bedrock to my teaching.

My thinking has expanded in several ways since the ramp project. I've always winced, remembering that I didn't know Sophie's dad used a wheelchair. In my early years of teaching, I kept a careful distance from the children's families, seeing the classroom as my personal terrain. The ramp project began in the first weeks of the school year, when my focus was on establishing myself as the children's teacher. I sent notes home explaining my background and my teaching philosophy and my expectations for "family participation," but I didn't invite much genuine exchange with families. I clearly had missed some significant learning about the children's lives.

In the years since the ramp project, I've worked consciously to change the ways in which I think about and enter into relationship with children's families. In the ramp story, I wrote that "it was an effort for me to let go of my position as the only adult in the classroom and be ready to add to or change my ideas, to truly welcome parents' involvement." That's exactly right—I put up roadblocks to relationships with families. Over time, I've come to recognize that I need to dismantle those barriers in order to know the children deeply and authentically and to offer myself genuinely and fully. Now I work to create relationships with families that extend far beyond sharing classroom housekeeping duties and chaperoning field trips and into the terrain of shared reflection about children's conversations and play and shared planning of responsive curriculum.

The other significant change in my thinking involves the focus of the project itself. I was quick to throw my hat into the ring with the children: "Yes, let's build a ramp!" We moved full-speed ahead to learn about elements of construction and in the process raced past opportunities to linger with relationships and with social justice issues. Now I'd ask bigger questions right away: What makes a school fair or unfair? How can we learn about what's fair for people who use wheelchairs? I'd hook us up with disability rights activists, to locate the children's passion about fairness in a larger context, and link them to a community of activists. I'd work more closely with the church that housed our program, not just telling them that "we want to build a ramp," but slowing down to listen to the stories of people in the church: Were there members of the congregation who used wheelchairs? How did they navigate the building? I'd focus less on construction and more on people and relationships among people and people's work for fairness.

It's encouraging to look back at this story and see the seeds of my current teaching practices and ways of thinking just beginning to take root. And it's encouraging to notice how I've changed since the ramp project—encouraging to see my understandings and my teaching growing and evolving. The seeds of documentation have grown into reflective, responsive teaching. The seeds of emergent curriculum have grown into an emphasis on in-depth studies of big ideas rather than on topical projects. And the seeds of collaboration with families have grown into a commitment to opening up my relationships with families. I hope that, should I revisit this reflection in another decade, I'd find more growth, more change, more evolution in my thinking and my teaching.

Share Your Reflections with Ann

Write a letter to Ann at APeloReflect@gmail.com with your reflections on how she was learning to negotiate the curriculum to respect the children's themes as well as uphold her own values. Consider including your thoughts about the following:

- What changes did you hear in Ann's thinking as she reflects on this story a decade later?
- What new insights did she gain about the children's perspectives?
- How did she try to integrate her antibias goals into her curriculum?
- How did she work with others in her community to pursue the children's interests?

An Inspirational Story

Like Ann Pelo, Rukia Monique Rogers is serious about
following the children's ideas. As you read the story, notice
how Rukia acknowledges the friction between her perspectives and the children's. Yet, by holding a strong image of the
children, she expands her understandings of the teaching and
learning process.

The Power of the Princess: Our Many Investigations

Rukia Monique Rogers, Child Care Teacher and College Student

This is a tale of learning how to teach out of love, yet empowering young children to produce thoughts of their own, to claim a world of their own. The path of this story has not been smooth. Instead, it has been a cycle of inquiry that emerged from the voices of preschoolers who were unwavering in their interest in princesses, combined with my initial reluctance to hear those voices. In this process of friction between their interests and mine, I had to rethink my image of the child. I had to reexamine my role as a teacher and take ownership of my potential as a researcher, a coach, and a nurturer. My decision to pursue this project came from deep love for the children I worked alongside and from my personal hopes and aspirations for them.

Learning to Listen

One year in my preschool class, I became keenly aware of the interest many children had in princesses and all that entails. I heard their stories of happily ever after, witnessed their Disney-driven play, and saw it in their numerous drawings. Initially, I chose to pay little or no attention to it. As a class, we engaged in much deeper and grander investigations, or so I thought.

I clearly remember the turning point for me. We were sitting at the lunch table. I could hear the girls chattering about princesses.

Jordyn: Well, I want to be Cinderella, and you can be Snow White.
Emily: I cannot be Snow White! (spoken as she rubbed her soft olive skin)
Her skin is white as snow. You can't be Cinderella either. Her skin is white too.

My ears perked up, and I began to listen. My class, and particularly these children, represented every tint and shade of brown. So, I wondered, who could they be? How would their self-image unfold?

The children's conversation challenged me to think about the materials and images in the classroom and whether they represented the children's identities. Faced with my unwillingness to listen, perhaps the only alternative they had was commercially manufactured concepts of beauty. I wanted to offer the children a different image of what a princess could look like. I began this process by fashioning an invitation of carefully arranged materials to elicit the idea of a beautifully dressed doll that was a woman of color (I had to create my own, as there were none to purchase) along with drawing tools and paper. Several of the children accepted this invitation to explore, studied the doll, and created a still life drawing. The children then discussed her color and what colors of paint they would need to create her hue of brown. For several days this same group of girls experimented with color mixing in order to create the doll's skin color, as well as to match their own. This theme of identity surfaced time and again as the children, both boys and girls, eventually invented princesses using their own likenesses.

Learning to Collaborate

Seeking other perspectives, I began to share my observations and questions with colleagues. We found other children and staff in our school who were interested in princesses, and we began to meet both formally and informally to share our ideas. It was during these conversations that I began to realize the many possibilities of this theme. We brainstormed and combed over the specific observations of children and how the children expressed this interest in their own way through storytelling, painting, clay, drawing, messages, dramatic play, and block play. The concept web we created to help guide our thinking was filled with questions and ideas as the path for moving forward.

In our classroom, we met with parents every couple of months to share ideas and observations, and to set forth the upcoming projections. These meetings were opportunities to draw on the perspectives of parents. Several of the parents expressed concern over exploring the topic of princesses and commercialism and how this process would lead to learning. Our relationships with the parents held us together, allowing for open, honest, and challenging conversations despite conflicting values. We used our documentation of the children's story's as a way to further engage the parents in dialogues about our thinking as well as the ways that exploring princesses could lead to learning and address greater concepts. One parent commented:

When I first discovered that my daughter, Madeline, was going to explore princesses at the Clifton School with her teachers and classmates, I was disappointed. We wanted Maddy to be a free thinker who didn't have to wait for a prince to feel complete. We hoped she would read books about strong, competent women. But Madeline loved princesses, and this topic came up at every turn.

I visited the Clifton School and looked at the princess documentation that had already begun to adorn the walls of Madeline's classroom. There were drawings and photos of young and old princesses, some of them with blemishes. I saw documented conversations about modern princesses and modern princess story endings. It was then that I realized my husband and I had done exactly the opposite of what we should have been doing when we banned the topic of princesses from our home. This project wasn't really about princesses. It was about dismantling stereotypes, creating a new scenario for the modern woman, feeling comfortable in one's own skin.

Through negotiations with the children's families and each other, we were able to collectively see the benefits of pursuing a greater understanding of the children's ideas and theories as they related to princesses. I took up the challenge to be intentional about researching the emerging ideas surrounding princesses, not only to study the children's interest but to offer another perspective and some complexity. To make my intention transparent to the children, the parents, and the community. I wrote the following statement.

Our popular culture is saturated with fairytales of princesses, princes, castles, knights, and dragons. Images from these tales can be found in popular media, books, toys, clothing, and so forth. Understandably, the children's attraction to this theme is an insatiable interest that we've observed and documented over the year. This is evident in their drawings, play, and representations of castles. As teachers, how do we support this interest and yet encourage them not just to consume popular culture, but to claim it as their own? How do the children use stories to express their interest? How do the children define beauty? What are their concepts of gender roles? Why are the children drawn to princesses? Is it the power or the prestige?

Exploring Children's Theories about Emotions

Our brainstorming led us toward many possibilities from which we had to make choices. We were interested in the children's correlation between one's outer appearance and how one behaved. Those considered attractive, represented by the princess standard, were kind and pure, whereas those considered unattractive, such as the wicked stepmother, were viewed as evil. We also noticed the children viewed with disdain behaviors expressing the natural emotions of anger and frustration.

Emily: They [princesses] never become angry. They are so kind and pretty that they forget to get angry.

Lindsey: If a person gets angry, they're not a real princess.

Challenging the Children to Rethink Their Theories

We teachers explored the idea of challenging the children's thinking. It was in the language of storytelling that we could hear the children's beliefs surrounding emotions and behavior. So I chose to retell the classic story of Cinderella during our morning meeting and offer an alternative ending. The prince came to place the glass slipper on Cinderella's foot—only this time it didn't fit, and Cinderella got angry and stormed off.

The children were stunned. Emily remarked, "It was like I was shot in my heart."

We continued to explore different ways to tell princess stories, such as from the perspectives of the stepsisters and the prince. Soon the children began to invent and perform their own tales.

Exploring and Challenging Children's Concepts about Beauty

To seek a better understanding of the children's perception of beauty, we offered them various magazines and asked them to show us "Who could be a princess." We noticed that the children's selections paid little attention to skin color or tone. Instead, they viewed imperfections, blemishes, wrinkles, and signs of aging as negative and not attractive.

Camryn: She's too old! Look at those lines around her eyes.
Jordyn: She's wrinkled.

Because the children expressed a belief that women with wrinkles or blemishes could not be princesses, I decided to invite a small group to study some photos of Princess Margaret of England throughout her life. I wanted to engage the children in a conversation about the process of aging. Without sharing all the photos at once, I placed on the table a picture of Princess Margaret on her wedding day.

Camryn: She's prettier than any other princess.

I then offered another picture of Princess Margaret slightly older.

Jordyn: She's got on different clothes, and she's older.
Camryn: She has a line around her nose; this is when she's getting older.
Ms. Rukia: But you stated before that princesses don't get old.
Noa: Yes, they do sometimes.

I proceeded to show them another picture of an elderly Princess Margaret in a wheelchair, and Camryn began to laugh.

Ms. Rukia: Why are you laughing?
Camryn: We laugh at people when they get old.
Jordyn: That's not nice!

There was a long silent pause.

Camryn: We shouldn't laugh at princesses because of the way they look.
Jordyn: That might hurt their feelings.
Camryn: We shouldn't laugh at anyone because of the way they look.

My Learning and the Children's Learning

This process of investigating princesses spanned a year and expanded to the study of castles, the creation of books and plays, and much more. The children acquired new skills and knowledge in the process. But the most significant learning I saw was that the scripted idea about a princess had forever changed. Some princesses decided not to get married. Other princesses had the power to fly. The children's drawings no longer represented prefabricated princess characters but instead expanded to include representations of a pregnant Indian princess draped with a sari and mehndi. I found joy in their emerging ideas and learning. I also recognized how much I had learned and expanded my thinking about the teaching and learning process. I began to take ownership of my role as a teacher. I learned not to ignore children's ideas that annoyed me. I saw how I could provoke the children into deeper thinking without putting them down or correcting them.

Share Your Reflections with Rukia

Write a letter to Rukia at RRogersReflect@gmail.com with your reflections on how she was learning to negotiate the curriculum to respect the children's themes as well as uphold her own values. Consider including your thoughts about the following:

- What did she learn about herself?

- How did she use the environment and materials to further the children's themes?

- What new insights did she learn about the children's perspectives?

- How did she negotiate her values with the children and their families?

▸ *Practice What You've Learned*

Practice Responding to Children's Themes

To practice applying the ideas and skills in this chapter, read each of the following projects and decide which responses involve a child-centered approach.

Samantha's Project

Samantha is working in the carpentry area. She puts a piece of wood in the vise, measures it, and saws off a piece of wood about six inches long. Then she uses that piece to measure and cut another piece the same size. Removing the wood from the vise, she places the two cut pieces on top of each other and, with two hands, begins hammering a nail through the top piece. She hits the nail head every third or fourth try and periodically stops to reposition the wood, which slides around the table. When she realizes the nail isn't attaching the two pieces together, she leaves the area. The next time you notice her, she's back in the carpentry area with a bottle of glue. Having attached the two pieces of wood together, she is now gluing some Styrofoam circles on the side.

1. What developmental themes and learning domains are apparent in Samantha's play? From your observation, describe her approach to learning, the ideas she is exploring, and the skills she is using and practicing.

2. Consider the role the teacher plays in each of the following responses. Use these questions to help you evaluate the following five possible teacher responses: How might Samantha feel or interpret this response? Does this response help the teacher learn more about Samantha?

a. The teacher says, "Oh, what a nice car you are making."

b. The teacher says, "I noticed how you used the vise to hold the wood while you measured and sawed. What did you discover makes it easier to cut?"

c. The teacher says, "There's paint in the art area. Would you like to paint your car?"

d. The teacher asks, "How many wheels does a car need?"

e. The teacher stands back and watches to see what Samantha is going to do next.

3. What response would you like to see happen?

A Closer Look

Did you notice that the teacher response with descriptive language and a related question (b) is the most pertinent to the child's interest? The other statements and questions (responses a, c, and d) almost seem trivial and simplistic. When is it appropriate for a teacher to watch and say nothing, as reflected in the last description (e)? If a teacher observes with a purpose, he gathers more information for curriculum planning and appropriate interventions in the future.

Mario's Project

Mario seems to be enjoying himself in the sand area. He started filling a baby bottle, first using his hand as a scoop and then using a cup. He then turned the baby bottle over and used it as a scoop. Now, using a funnel as a scoop, he is noticing that the sand can run out both ends of the funnel into the bottle.

1. What developmental themes and learning domains are apparent in Mario's play? From your observation, describe his approach to

learning, the ideas he is exploring, and the skills he is using and practicing.

2. Consider the role the teacher plays in each of the following responses. Use these questions to help you evaluate the following five possible teacher responses: How might Mario feel or interpret this response? Does this response help the teacher learn more about Mario?

   a. The teacher picks up a bigger funnel and asks, "Which of these funnels is bigger, yours or mine?"

   b. The teacher picks up a funnel and tries using it just like Mario, thinking to herself, "Maybe if I get a container and funnel and use them the same way he does, Mario will talk to me about his play."

   c. The teacher says to Mario, "You figured out how to get sand into that bottle two different ways! What have you discovered about what works best?"

   d. The teacher says, "Mario, are you making a birthday cake?"

   e. The teacher says, "Mario, why don't you pour your sand over this truck and bury it?"

3. What response would you like to see happen?

A Closer Look

Responses b and c take into consideration Mario's interests at the sand table. Often a teacher's ideas and interest have no meaning to the child (e.g., responses a, d, and e). Following the child's lead starts to impact the way you respond.

LaToya's Project

LaToya seems to be hanging around the edges of the dress-up corner beauty parlor play as if she would like to join in. She is holding a purse and some rollers and is watching the "beauty parlor lady" and the girl in the chair getting her hair done.

1. What developmental themes and learning domains are apparent in LaToya's play? From your observation, describe her approach to learning, the ideas she is exploring, and the skills she is using and practicing.

2. Consider the role the teacher plays in each of the following responses. Use these questions to help you evaluate the following five possible teacher responses: How might LaToya feel or interpret this response? Does this response help the teacher learn more about LaToya?

   a. The teacher says to the other children, "LaToya wants to play. Why don't you be nice and invite her to play with you?"

   b. The teacher thinks to herself, "Maybe if I get a purse and some rollers, I could say, 'Hi, I'd sure like to get my hair fixed too.' I'll wait to see if LaToya wants to keep watching or if she wants to join in the play."

   c. The teacher says, "I see you have a purse and some rollers with you. Are you going to fix the doll's hair?"

   d. The teacher says, "Only four people are allowed in the dress-up area, LaToya. You'll have to find somewhere else to play until someone leaves this area."

   e. The teacher says, "Hey, beauty parlor lady, you have another customer waiting for her appointment."

3. What response would you like to see happen?

A Closer Look

The first response, (a), doesn't give LaToya the scaffolding she needs to join in the play. Responses b, c, and e, however, provide a scaffold while still allowing LaToya to take the necessary steps to join the play. Response (d) is focused on a rule, not the child. Coaching gives the teacher an opportunity to observe and encourage involvement while allowing for self-initiative and respecting the child's preferences and intentions.

Notes about Your Theme Planning

Reflect on your use of themes in your curriculum planning. The following questions will get you started.

Look over your last few months of curriculum. Has your planning provided for the children's developmental themes or only topical themes?

What changes would you like to make?

_____

_____

_____

_____

_____

_____

_____

_____

_____

_____

What is your next step?

_____

_____

_____

_____

_____

_____

_____

_____

_____

_____

Putting Academic Learning in Its Place

▶ Beginning Reflections

Think back on your earliest memories of excitement about learning.
Maybe it was sitting on your grandma's lap reading along with her as
she read your favorite book over and over again. Perhaps you pretended
to be a scientist experimenting by mixing dirt and water to make mud.
Or you became a biologist fascinated by the insects you studied in your
yard. Maybe you remember how proud you felt counting the candles on
your birthday cake.

Record those memories here:

_____

_____

_____

_____

_____

_____

_____

_____

Now think back about your formal school experiences. What did school offer you that strengthened your identity as an eager learner? What experiences undermined your eagerness to learn?

_____

_____

_____

_____

_____

_____

_____

_____

Share examples with someone else to see if they had similar or different experiences.

How can these early learning experiences influence your work with children?

_____

_____

_____

_____

_____

_____

Historically the idea of school readiness has somehow focused on getting children ready for school, not on getting our schools ready for children. Parents, teachers, employers, and policy makers want children to quickly become productive members of society. But if you look closely and listen to the children themselves, they are bounding into the world very ready and eager to learn. Their active bodies, minds, and imaginations want to discover and understand everything. Children are eager to learn and show their competence. How can we get our schools ready for them?

Gloria thinks there are some pretty cool things to do at preschool. Today she is continually rearranging a large collection of blocks on the floor with her new friend, Raoul, telling him how she's building a city on the moon and has to get it right "so the space patrol has a safe place to land." She leans her face down parallel to the floor as she runs her hands across a collection of blocks she has arranged into a large square. "Nope, still got edges where they might fall in. I got to get it measured even." Suddenly her teacher, Miss Rebecca, calls Gloria to come to the art table to make an alphabet book. Gloria wishes she didn't have to leave her moon city and her new friend Raoul, who seems to want to play with her, but it's the second time she's been called. If she has to leave the block area, she'd rather eat a snack or go find that book with the pictures of the moon. But yesterday Gloria's teacher showed her the schedule on the wall, and she can tell it's not time for that now. Gloria goes to the art table and hastily glues pictures onto the papers with letters her teacher gives her. "Now you'll be able to sing the alphabet song with your book," Miss Rebecca says.

If we could peek inside Gloria's head, we might possibly hear her singing, "Now I know my ABCs, but they don't mean a thing to me."

The terms *preschool* and *Head Start* suggest that children need group settings where adults give them a jump start for the world of academics and for the behavior that is expected in school. Indeed, all the recent brain research suggests that the earliest years are when children get wired for learning everything—physical, language, social, emotional, and cognitive development. We've learned that all of this happens best in the context of trusting, respectful relationships, from which children come to see themselves as lovable and able learners. So how do we teach children the skills they will need to be successful in school and life while still honoring their childhood endeavors and helping them enjoy living in the here and now?

Preparing Children for a World We Cannot Yet See

Singer Tom Hunter (2008) wrote:

> This world is changing so fast we can't see what's coming before
>   it arrives.
> To think passing tests will get our kids ready is a gamble we
>   play with their lives.
> How can we prepare our children for a world we cannot yet see?
> I say we work hard so they can become as human as they can be.

Tom's song reminds us how fast the world is changing, requiring us to figure out how to prepare our children for a world we cannot yet see. What a challenge for teachers! Tom's solution is that we need to teach children to be as human as they can be. Children need adult guidance to help them build conceptual understandings, develop positive values, and grow into responsible citizens of the world. Other educators suggest that for children to be successful in school and their future lives, curriculum has to be crafted to help them think through problems and solutions. Valuable research in the early childhood field suggests that focusing our work on cultivating desirable dispositions and approaches to learning is one of the most important tasks for teachers.

Focus on Approaches to Learning

Children are natural learners, but they need to have their internal, intrinsic motivation to be lifelong learners reinforced. You see their eagerness to learn beginning in infancy. Supporting this eagerness should be our real readiness agenda! As children become preschoolers, initial academic experiences should fill them with joy, not dread or boredom. Watch them for signs of eager desire to learn, and look for everyday ways to support these dispositions as you embed literacy, math, and science into everything children do. These concepts and skills are not taught as separate lessons, but are discovered and developed as children play, eat, and enter transitions. Try documenting examples for the questions that follow. In an environment with lots of interesting choices for children, it won't take long for you to fill up your paper with specific accounts of the indicators that children are developing the approaches to learning that are the foundation for success in school and life. You'll see these indicators in children of all ages, from infants all the way through pre-K.

- What signs do you see that a child is motivated to learn something?

- What do you see a child doing that demonstrates she is being persistent in productive ways?

- Can you see indications of a child being a flexible problem solver?

- Do you see a child showing he can tolerate some frustration or delayed gratification?

- What do you see a child doing that displays an ability to plan, focus, and hold attention?

When you observe children with these approaches to learning, they are communicating a readiness for more direct coaching. This coaching will support children as they attend to bigger conceptual ideas and learn more specific skills to achieve their goals and academic success. You can strengthen these useful dispositions by keeping learning meaningful and fun.

Focus on Intellectual Development Not Just Standards

Lilian Katz (2008a) makes a helpful distinction between academic learning and intellectual development. She reminds us that academic lessons are often focused on discrete bits of information taken out of context and often taught with an emphasis on memorization or reciting the correct answer. Intellectual development, on the other hand, focuses on "the life of the mind in its fullest sense" (Katz 2008b). This includes everything from aesthetic and moral sensibilities to the exploration of ideas and the skills of reasoning and inquiry. Academic information is important at some point in the learning process, of course, but we want to encourage young children to be active learners, not just passive receivers of information. This requires that we help children find their questions, connect ideas, and understand the bigger picture of academic disciplines.

Address Standards and Academic Learning in Everyday Activities

Child-centered, play-oriented early childhood educators have been hesitant to embrace the growing emphasis on working with state-mandated early learning standards. Teachers fear an inappropriate push-down academic curriculum will rob children of their childhoods. But Judy Graves and Susan MacKay (2009) offer an expanded perspective for us to consider. If we take the best intentions of state departments of education to heart, we see that the standards have the goal of ensuring that all children, regardless of their backgrounds and economic circumstances, receive a quality education.

In a world driven by information technology, educators need to rethink the nature of academic learning. What will be useful for children as they move into later schooling and adulthood? Children benefit from coaching that helps them understand *why* reading, math, and science knowledge might be useful to them. They need us to guide them in *how to think* through learning tasks, *how to find* information, and *why* seeking multiple perspectives is worthwhile.

Children deserve opportunities to learn more about academic disciplines. As we strive to protect childhood and developmentally appropriate practices, we should remember that children are eager to learn academic subjects when they are offered in ways that include active exploration and the opportunity to construct understandings. This approach enhances deeper learning, as opposed to just a recitation of memorized facts. Teachers must take up the challenge of learning more about the thinking processes, skills, and content of different academic domains. Sometimes this occurs right alongside the children, even as you strive to keep a few steps ahead of their growing knowledge in particular areas. Whatever your choices for teaching academics, you should focus on the learning as well as the teaching process. When you offer any kind of lessons or planned learning activities, do so in meaningful ways using the context of children's daily routines and play in your program.

Literacy Learning and Meaningful Print in the Environment

For years the early childhood field has emphasized the importance of creating a print-rich environment to support children's literacy development. Too often, however, this has resulted in a cluttered arrangement of labels and signs all over the classroom unlike anything you might find in a real-world context. As you seek to provide a print-rich environment, keep asking yourself, "How can I make this as meaningful as it would be if found in the real world?" For instance, it is common and useful to put names on diaper bins, cubbies, mailboxes, and personal items, but where in the real world do you see words labeling things such as windows, chairs, and rugs? People might need labels on things such as exits and bathrooms, their spice jars, and leftovers in the refrigerator, but not their lamps, tables, and computers. How does helpful signage in our homes and communities translate into what is meaningful to label in your classroom? If the idea of "print rich" becomes "print overstimulation," it is no longer useful to children or motivating them to pay attention to associating those labels with the objects they represent.

Surrounding children with print doesn't necessarily prepare them for academic success. Recent studies have refocused our attention on three other areas that are predictors of school success, beginning with infants and toddlers:

- expanding the vocabulary you use with children
- reading to children
- modeling the value and enjoyment of reading

As you plan your environment and projects and engage children in conversations, you will find you can address these predictors of school success. The following pages offer some examples of meaningful activities to get you started.

In your everyday activities with children, reinforce *why* reading and writing are useful and enjoyable. This will promote involvement and encourage their desire to acquire the fine-motor skills and conventions of reading and writing.

When children understand that literacy learning involves decoding symbols, they can come to enjoy it as much as they do I Spy games.

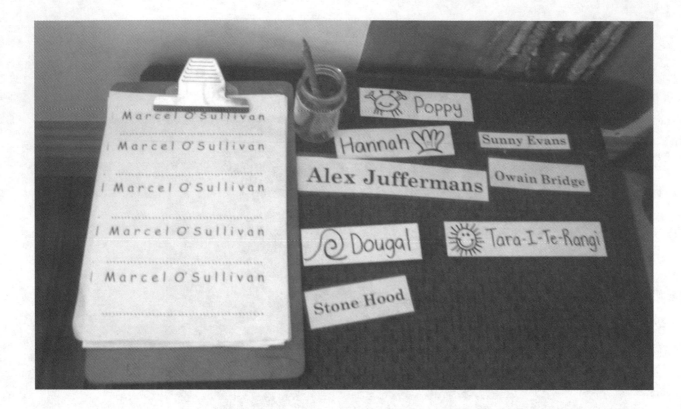

When they see the value of writing something down so that it can be read back and remembered, children appreciate the function and power of the written word and want to master it. As children see you turn to reference materials such as the class roster, the lunch menu, or instructions for assembling some new furniture, you can narrate how this written material is helpful to you. When they hear you describe what you text or type on the computer, they see firsthand the power of the written word to communicate ideas and messages to others.

"I'm going to find the diaper basket that has your name on it. Here it is. It says, R-i-c-k-y. Those letter sounds spell your name, Ricky."

"I'm going to look at this list of everyone's first and last names so I can remember them."

"Let's see what our menu says we are having for lunch today."

"I want to figure out how to put this table together, so I'm going to read the pictures and instructions that came with it."

"I'm going to send your dad an e-mail with the story of how carefully you made that city skyscraper in the block area. Should we attach some photos, too?"

You can also begin to involve the children in adding to your reference material.

"Beside each of your names, I'm going to write the names of who's in your family. That will help me remember who's important to you."

"Let's make a chart of everyone's favorite foods so we know who will smile when I read the menu each day."

"Let's draw and write out the directions for how we made this play-dough so you can take it home and help your family learn how to make it."

You will want to have a book area, writing center, mailboxes, and technology in your classroom, but think of all the other places in the room where reference books and writing tools also would be useful. (Hint: Think about where books, pens, papers, magazines, reference materials, and information technology can help you in your home.)

Use Routines for Meaningful Writing

Even before children can read or write, involve them in functional literacy routines. Making a mark or scribble to stand for letters in a word is an appropriate starting place. If children protest, saying they don't know how to write, tell them just to pretend they know how. One of the biggest motivators for children is to learn how to write and recognize their names and those of their family members, pets, and friends. Find ways to involve children in name writing and name reading many times a day. Encourage them to put their names on their work and on lists you use to track where kids are or what they are doing. Likewise, encourage them to write notes, perhaps with drawings, to send to their family members or put in classroom mailboxes. If you have computers in your classroom, set up e-mail boxes for each child. You can use picture symbols to guide them in any of these tasks.

Regularly Make Homemade Books

Expand the collection of books you have around your room with homemade books that include photos and texts about what the children have been doing. You can reformat some of your required documentation into child-friendly language and make it available as reading material for the children. You can also make books from stories children dictate and illustrate. These homemade books can be put in binders, mounted on card stock, or bound in any number of ways. You can also make and print them directly from the computer with word processing software and other readily available applications such as RealeWriter. Remember, homemade books are useful for infants and toddlers as well as older children.

Topic ideas for homemade books include the following:

- people who are special in my life
- how we use materials in different parts of the room
- how we've learned to be friends
- experts in our room
- special projects or field trips we have been doing
- curiosities and big questions we have
- how we take care of the earth
- welcome books and farewell books as children join and leave the program

Some of your homemade books can include book-writing conventions such as biographies of the authors, a dedication from the author, a title page, a table of contents, and so forth.

Basic Ideas to Start With

Your task as a teacher is not to keep adding lessons to your schedule, but rather to thread academic learning into every activity. Keep an eye out for where a child or group could benefit from some direct instruction or coaching to better achieve some goals they seem to have. Listen for their questions rather than always having them focused on yours. Likewise, try to avoid what is referred to as instruction in "silos"— disconnected, out-of-context lessons that have little intrinsic meaning for children. Above all, have fun with learning games, and never convey the idea that you are testing children as you explore letters, numbers, and science concepts. You want to keep children intrinsically motivated to master what will make them successful in the world of adults.

Any number of resources with literacy, math, and science activities are available to early childhood educators. Study and adapt the ones that seem most child-centered to you. The lists of ideas below can help you start thinking about ways to integrate "serious" curriculum into activities that you may already do with your children.

Early literacy specialist Evelyn Lieberman (1985) offers six areas of literacy skills to cultivate in children, with the following tips for embedding them into your regular activities with children. Depending on the age of the children and their language skills, the role of the teacher is somewhat different. Children of all ages need to hear teachers narrating, raising questions, describing details, singing, reading, and using a wide vocabulary. As children get older, teachers can encourage them to use these same skills.

Narrative Skills

Narrative skills help children to develop the ability to describe things and events and to tell stories.

- Tell or listen to family stories.
- Ask children to retell stories from books, movies, or experiences.
- Ask children to recall the day's activities.
- Take dictation after an event or activity.
- Tell a story with props or manipulatives.
- Make up class stories.
- Make books together.
- Say or sing nursery rhymes.
- Play I Spy games.

Vocabulary Building

As children build their vocabulary, they begin knowing the names of things. As they learn synonyms and other vocabulary, they broaden the range of their ability to communicate more exactly.

- Listen to and encourage children's conversations, restating their ideas in different words.

- A children to describe pictures or tell what's happening in stories.

- Encourage children to use new words.

- Use unfamiliar words, and explain their meaning in a context that children can understand.

- Define unfamiliar words while reading or talking.

- Ask children to explain what specific words mean.

- Ask children to think of ten different words to describe an object.

- Read books that introduce new concepts.

- Plan activities to introduce new words (e.g., building ramps, during which you can use words like incline planes, angle, slant, pitch).

Print Motivation

Print motivation involves expanding a child's interest in and enjoyment of books and reading materials, while also stimulating the child's interest in writing.

- Place clipboards, paper, and pens around the room.

- Put sign-making materials in the block area.

- Have children write their names.

- Involve children in making classroom lists.

- Set up mailboxes and a writing center.

- Frequently write letters and e-mail with the children.

- Have others (e.g., family members, people in your program or from the community) write letters to the children to be read aloud.

- Encourage children to write in play situations.

- Let children choose books for you to read.

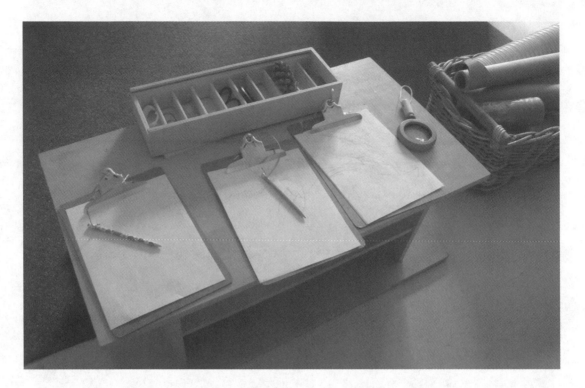

- Put books in all learning centers around the room.

- Include time to read in your schedule.

- Use reading to help children accomplish tasks.

- Ask children to sign in for attendance.

- Read a big book to a child or the group.

- Use an interactive chart for songs or transitions.

Developing Print Awareness

Print awareness involves children understanding basic concepts about books and print. These skills involve learning how to handle a book, paging from the front to the back of a book, following written words, and other visual and motor skills involved in reading.

- Point out authentic environmental print (stop signs, food packaging, license plates, etc.).

- Let children turn the pages of the book while you read.

- Point to words as you read books to kids.

- Talk about the concept of "word."

- Explain that you read print, not pictures.

- Move your finger from left to right under words when reading aloud.

- Ask children to find familiar words while you read to them.

- Sing the ABC song as you point to written alphabet letters.

Letter Knowledge

Letter knowledge is much more than simply reciting the alphabet. It involves understanding that letters are different from each other, that letters have names, and that specific sounds are associated with each letter.

- Spell children's names out loud as you write or point them out.

- Talk about the letters in children's names that sound alike or start with the same letter.

- Talk about what is the same and what is different between two things (e.g., this block is curved; this block is straight).

- Point out and name letters while reading alphabet books, signs, or labels.

- Use magnetic letters.

- Make letters from playdough.

- Assemble alphabet puzzles.

- Sing the ABC song.

- Count the letters in names or words.

Phonemic Awareness

Phonemic awareness involves developing the ability to hear and play with smaller sounds in words. Through phonemic awareness, children begin to understand that words are made up of a number of blended sounds.

- Sing rhyming songs.
- Play at rhyming words and sounds.
- Clap the beat in songs.
- Clap syllables in names.
- Clap syllables in words.
- Read poetry.
- Say or sing nursery rhymes.
- Talk about letter-sound correspondence.
- Talk about letter-sound similarities.

Bilingual Language Learning

At one time or another, most early childhood programs include children whose first language is not English. It is important to work closely with the families of these children. You need to ensure that as the children begin to acquire English proficiency, they continue to master their home language as well. This keeps them tied to their families and culture even as they integrate into other settings. A number of valuable resources are available on bilingual education, English language learning, and multilingual classrooms. For a comprehensive overview of the elements to consider in developing programs in more than one language, you can read *Soy Bilingüe: Language, Culture, and Young Latino Children* by Sharon Cronin and Carmen Sosa Massó (2003).

Working with translators may be useful, but remember that mere translation is not the same as fully developing proficiency in more than one language. The United States is one of the only countries in the world where most education doesn't include learning to be proficient in more than one language. Given the global world we are preparing children to live in and the huge influx of new immigrants in many communities in our country, we should be sharpening our skills at providing bilingual classrooms. Brain research tells us that we most easily learn languages when we are young and our brains are developing their distinct auditory pathways. All children benefit from learning a second language.

The concept of literacy involves understanding the particular codes, relationships, and language structures for communicating different ideas. How can we support young children in becoming literate in the areas of technology, music, visual arts, and even finances? Children are usually curious about, if not eager to engage in these areas. We should consider ways to deepen their understandings in these topics.

Mathematical Learning and Literacy

To many, mathematics seems like a different language and something needed only for school learning. You, however, can help even the youngest children see that math is everywhere and relates to not only our everyday activities but also to learning other academic subjects such as science, art, and music. The National Council of Teachers of Mathematics (NCTM) reminds us that there are two kinds of math to pay attention to in our teaching—thinking math and content math. Here are some starting activities adapted from NCTM.

Thinking Math

Learning to think like a mathematician involves problem solving, communication, reasoning, and connections. Consider simple activities like these:

- Ask children to help you organize things on shelves to experiment with relative size and shape and how much more room the larger items take than the smaller ones.

- Set up pouring activities at the sensory table using different sized cups to help children discover which cup will hold the most.

- Have children make diagrams or draw pictures to represent numbers, for instance, how many children like pizza and how many don't like pizza.

- Involve children in setting the table for activities or snacks, planning for how many will be able to sit together comfortably.

Content Math

Appropriate math content for young children explores things such as patterns and relationships, number sense, estimation, measurement, spatial relations, and geometry. Try simple things like these:

- Create pattern games with blocks, beads, or other suitable materials.

- Create pattern games with sounds, clapping, or chants.

- Practice ordering materials from shortest to longest, smallest to largest, and so forth.

- Play I Spy games, looking for patterns in pictures, quilts, and animal skins.

- Explain what numbers are used for within different contexts to help children learn that numbers are used to describe quantities as well as relationships and measurements (e.g., keeping score, using the phone, finding an address, learning the steps in doing something).

- Count real things during the day to help children better understand numbers.

- Point to objects or hold up fingers one at a time as you say numbers when counting.

- Provide lots of opportunities for climbing in and out, over and under so that children experience themselves in space.

- Offer hands-on experiences for learning geometric shapes (e.g., blocks, puzzles, cookie cutters).

- Find geometric shapes in everyday walks on streets, in signs, and in art.

- Involve children in measuring things, narrating as you go and using conventional tools (e.g., measuring tapes, spoons, cups) as well as nonconventional measuring tools (e.g., string, cereal boxes).

- Play games like "Who can stand on one foot longer?" or "How many laps can you run around the playground before this timer goes off?" to help children develop a sense of measuring time.

- Connect math vocabulary such as "more than" and "less than" during activities in which children experiment with making estimations and predictions.

Scientific Literacy and Learning

In the first five years of life, children are naturally curious and wonder about what things are called, how they work, and why things happen. They are not only learning about the world, but also learning about learning. Children develop a "scientific mind" as they learn to collect information, fit it into what they already know, and figure out how to use what they know.

Teachers should develop both a disposition to be curious and their own scientific minds.

Thinking Science

Scientific learning should not be limited to a particular "science time." Teachers can support scientific thinking and behaviors in children throughout the day. This begins through the materials you provide for exploration and experimentation. As children investigate and play, you can converse with them and communicate the vocabulary of scientific thinking as well as possible science content areas.

- "Can you feel that wet diaper on your skin? Let's see how a dry one feels."

- "When you shake the rattle, it makes a sound."

- "When you change the angle of that ramp on the blocks, you are thinking like the kind of scientist we call a *physicist*. The angle of the ramp is called the *incline*."

- "I noticed you are putting drops of two different colors in the play-dough. That's what a scientist we call a *chemist* does. What are you discovering?"

Create a classroom culture with routines, plans, and responses to children that encourage them to think like a scientist. Find ways to help children learn to

- wonder and ask questions;

- learn from their senses;

- observe closely and notice details;

- compare and sort by looking carefully;

- count and measure to make comparisons;

- experiment by trial and error, test predictions, and draw conclusions;

- be persistent and keep trying again and again;

- share their questions and ideas with others by describing, drawing, charting, demonstrating, and writing what they wonder and discover; and

- work together with others and have fun.

Science Skills and Processes

The skills and processes of inquiry and exploration are fundamental to all the sciences. You can adapt your classroom environment, routines, and materials to encourage questioning and investigation. And you can coach children in developing scientific processes and skills. Above all, remember not to rush or interrupt children; they need time to investigate, absorb, and repeat their experiments.

When children are developing scientific inquiry skills, they are becoming good observers and questioners. You can help them add the scientific processes of collecting, comparing, and representing what they see and the data they gather. Learning to analyze, synthesize, and make predictions involves learning to see patterns and relationships. You can talk naturally to children to encourage their grasp of the skills and processes of inquiry throughout the day. This is particularly useful with infants and toddlers who are preverbal. With preschoolers, you can suggest they answer questions such as the following:

- What do you notice about this object? What are you discovering as you try using it?

- What are you curious about?

- How are they the same? What do they have in common?

- How are they different? What distinguishes them from each other?

- What will happen if . . . ? Can you predict what might happen next?

- How do you think it might change if we . . . ? What is your guess or hypothesis?

- Let's be scientists, look closely, predict, compare, and document our findings.

- We can document our findings and report the evidence, or what we saw happen in our experiment.

- We can observe and discover what happens when we change some of the objects or factors in our experiments.

Content Science

As a teacher you can look for opportunities to develop children's understanding of scientific concepts in all content areas. Most early childhood education catalogs have books with ideas for activities related to the various concepts of science. As you use them in your teaching, remember children need to observe things firsthand as much as possible. The younger the children, the simpler and more concrete the activities need to be. Make sure your classroom has scientifically accurate books about animals and their environments, including field guides and fictional stories. Make sure you use, and encourage children to use, the precise language of science. Here are some examples of beginning ideas for the content area of physical science. Use them to get inspired about simple things you can offer and say for science concepts in other content areas.

- Explore and describe the attributes of common objects, for example, size, shape, color, weight, texture.

- Sort, group, or classify objects based on one or more properties.

- Explore ways materials can be changed by combining, freezing, melting, dissolving, or applying physical pressure through pushing, pulling, pounding, or stretching.

- Experiment with moving a variety of objects by rolling, spinning, or blowing; then describe observations such as fast, slow, back and forth, zigzag.

- With blocks and building materials, observe how changes in position or weight will impact balance.

- Use words such as motion, gravity, force, mass, weight, velocity, and speed as you observe and talk about actions with materials.

Technology Literacy Learning

One of the first considerations for teachers in promoting literacy learning with information technology is an exploration of *why* and *how* technology should be used in early childhood programs. In today's world, children already spend too much time in front of a screen. Instead, they should be engaged in active play, spending more time outdoors, and experiencing face-to-face interactions with their peers and adults. Rather than avoid technology, teachers should consider how it fits in with their goals for children and the way they believe children learn best.

In many early childhood centers, computers are loaded with so-called educational software that is just an entertaining form of work sheets. Large whiteboards are starting to crowd out space for block building, filling the classroom with a high-tech version of group recitation lessons guided by goofy characters. It's also becoming common to see teachers focused more on their technology than engaging with the children. Whether from perceived pressure to input documentation, complete assessment reports, or keep current with e-mail, teachers can be found more engrossed in technology tools rather than in what the children are doing.

Fancy technology gadgets can divert attention and precious dollars away from curriculum practices that focus on children generating their own ideas, learning about learning, and pursuing their developmental themes. Some kinds of technology can play a valuable role in children's learning, but it should enhance—not divert—their attention away from meaningful connections with other people and engagement with their own questions and pursuits.

Using Technology to Reflect Children's Lives

The majority of children come to early childhood programs exposed to, if not experienced with, digital cameras, smart phones, computers, and the Internet. Take advantage of their technological skill and knowledge base to further support the teaching approach promoted in this book.

- Give children cameras to use in documenting their own work.

- Show them the steps for setting up a computer file for downloading photos.

- Encourage them to produce books about their own activities with child-friendly software.

- Focus on the process of revisiting how they approached their work more than the product they produced with technology.

- Use whiteboards for the children to review something they have been doing, stopping to encourage them to predict what comes next, plan, who else they might involve in this play, what additional materials they might need, who they could send documentation to, and what other information they might want to seek out on the Internet.

- Develop a protocol of texting or tweeting to the children's families, near and far, with a provocative question accompanying a photo.

- Set up protected e-mail accounts or blogs for the children to e-dialogue with distant family members and friends in other places.

Analyzing a Role for Technology

Rather than routinely purchasing new technology and software for your program, first engage your colleagues, and hopefully the children's families, in considerations of where technology might enhance children's thinking, reflection, creativity, and collaborative learning.

First, brainstorm a list of specific approaches to learning you are trying to foster as you plan your environment, investigations, and projects for the children. Consider the discrete elements you might see when children are engaged in reflection, creativity, and collaboration. For instance, when children hear a story or look over documentation of their own work, they come up with ideas of new things to do or new people to include.

Review an existing observation or documentation story to explore possible places where some kind of technology might extend the opportunities for the desired approaches to learning and elements you have as goals for the children. For instance, if you see a group of children arguing over the best way to do something, you could give them a camera to take photos of each option. Then you could use each of the photos to guide the children in trying out each of the ideas, perhaps by projecting the photos on a whiteboard. You could also show them something on the Internet about their ideas.

An Inspirational Story

As you read the following story, notice how Evelyn Lieberman turned her curiosity as a mother into becoming a teacher-researcher seeking to better understand the specific steps children follow as they learn to write. As she consolidated her understandings from her research, she applied them in her everyday work with preschool children to make name writing and recognition a regular feature of her classroom.

From Scribbles to Name Writing

Evelyn Lieberman, Mother, Preschool Teacher, Teacher Educator, Researcher, Grandmother

In preschool my young son wrote backwards. Well, not just backwards; he wrote letters and words in "mirror writing." At first I just ignored this trait and learned to read it. However, in first grade his teachers became concerned this might be a sign of some dreaded neuro-developmental immaturity or, at the very least, imperfect penmanship. I did some research and found that mirror writing should be considered normal in preschool and should not be a cause for concern until around third grade. I was hooked. How did young children learn to write? What was the meaning of all those squiggles, circles, lines, and letters backward or out of order? What did preschoolers understand about written language?

Becoming a Researcher

I watched, wondered, and collected samples as my own five children, various cousins, and friends' children first tried to write. I became a preschool teacher, earned a master's degree, and taught child development and early childhood education classes. I read and reviewed and taught college classes about the developmental stages of growth and development. I consulted with preschool programs to make sure their curriculums were developmentally appropriate. Nevertheless, my dream of investigating how children came to understand written language was not realized until I chose a topic for my doctoral dissertation: "Name Writing and the Preschool Child."

I knew the developmental stages of cognitive, physical, social, and emotional development, the stages of drawing a picture of a person, throwing a ball, learning to sing, read, eat, talk, walk, and so on. However, when I tried to find information on "early childhood writing" in textbooks, the information was usually about "author's circles" and "journaling" for first graders, but nothing about understanding, recognizing, celebrating, or promoting emergent writing—all those marks children make before they construct adult-like letters or words.

As a "kid watcher," I knew that the first observable demonstration of young children's ability to use text as a symbol was drawing a picture of a person or writing the letters in their names. The question was how to describe or document this phenomenon. I devised a research plan. Once a month for an entire school year, I would tell children in several preschool classrooms to "write your name and draw a picture of yourself." These samples would be the data for my study. I soon had a large stack of 12 x 17 inch papers with all kinds of beautiful, colorful marks and drawings. How was I to make sense of them? Did they indicate a process that could be identified and described? Was there a developmental sequence of early writing?

Finding Meaning in My Data

After much thinking and playing around with ideas, I finally had my "Aha!" moment. I would write a sentence that described each writing sample. Next, I would sort the samples into similar piles, for example, all the scribbling samples in one pile, the horizontal zigzag lines in another, all the recogniz-able names in another, and so on. I discovered that I could describe every sample and that each sample fell into a group of similar samples. I now had sixteen statements that described all of the samples, but could the samples be aligned in a sequence?

Scribbling would be the first group, and the samples in which children could write their first and last names would be one of the final groups. Based on what I had seen while watching children write, I continued to intuitively arrange the remaining groups into an apparent logical order (see pages 210–11). I then had college students and teachers not involved in the study validate and confirm the accuracy of the sequence.

Now I had a replicable sequence. I could take any name-writing sample, look through the sequence, and find the sentence that described it. This turned out to be a time-consuming and rather tedious task. I wanted some-thing that teachers, students, parents, and others could easily use. How could I make it easier? Eventually I knew what to do. I arranged the sequence into a flow chart. I wrote each sentence on a note card and spread them out on my dining room table. After many tries and dead ends, I had a flow chart. Now anyone could look at a name-writing sample, quickly answer the questions in each box, and arrive at the description of that particular name-writing sample.

NAME WRITING SAMPLES

1. Scribbling. There are no recognizable figures or letter-like marks.

2. Letters or letter-like marks are mixed in with drawing.

Ashley   Bradley

Dustin   Max

3. Name writing is linear and separate from drawing.

Hillary

4. Name writing/autograph is a continuous horizontal zigzag line.

Ansonia   Mitchella

5. Horizontal zigzag line and separate letter-like marks.

Jovan   Anthony

6. Line of separate marks which may include letters from child's name and/or letter-like marks.

Jovanny   Shenna

7. Autograph contains placeholders, symbol(s) used "in place of" letters child cannot yet produce.

Brandon   Cynthia

8. Three or less marks which are first and/or last letters of name.

9. Letters from child's name, out of order, some missing or added.

10. Letters from child's name, in order, with some missing or added.

11. Same number of letters, letter-like marks, and/or placeholders as in child's name.

12. All letters are recognizable but some are not yet properly formed.

13. Correct number and form of all letters, but some may be out of order.

14. Letters in correct number, form and order.

15. Backwards, on two lines, or other creative placement or problem solving strategy.

16. First and last name.

Evelyn Lieberman Ph.D.
Name Writing and the
   Preschool Child
University of Arizona
© 1985

Applying What I Learned

Meanwhile, in my classroom I consciously added writing to my curriculum. I found that all I had to do was insert writing experiences into what was already happening. No specific writing lessons at 10:01. No group demonstrations on how to write. No expensive professional materials or guides to buy. I knew that just as all the children had gone from babbling to speaking sentences by listening to others talking, they would go from scribbles to writing by watching others write and experimenting with writing themselves. All they needed were pencils, crayons, chalk, paintbrushes—any writing instruments—and lots of paper, chalkboards, or other writing surfaces, and of course, time and encouragement from teachers and parents.

I decided that children should have the opportunity to recognize, read, or write their names at least ten times every day. For example, any day in my classroom, you might see Sammy walk into the room and "sign in" by either writing his name on a list or finding his name card in a box on the table. Then he would put his jacket in the cubby where he could see his picture and his name. He made a clay model and set it to dry on a piece of paper where I had written his name so he would know which one to paint tomorrow. At the easel, he watched as I wrote Aaron's name on his painting, saying each letter out loud as I wrote. Sammy wrote his name on his painting himself by making a horizontal zigzag line. I said, "Sammy, I love the way you wrote your name."

Sammy continued his literacy learning as the day went on. When he walked by the birthday chart, he paused and looked for his name. He found it, traced it with his finger, and said, "My birthday is coming soon." There was only one computer in the room, so Sammy checked to see whether his name was getting closer to the top of the computer wait list. There were letters to take home to parents, so Sammy looked for the envelope with his name on it and put it in his cubby. He looked for the journal with his name on the cover and drew some pictures. At the bottom of one, he made an S and a zigzag line. He said, "I signed my name," and I responded, "That's great! I like the way you write your name. Let's show it to your mother when she comes to pick you up."

Outside there were buckets of water and small paintbrushes so children could draw or write letters or their names on the hot cement and watch them evaporate. Sammy drew a picture of a person and wrote an *S* followed by a squiggly line. He watched and clapped as they disappeared. Lots of children wanted to swing, so I said, "We need to make a list to know whose turn is next." Sammy said, "We need pencil and paper," and ran off to get them. Later Sammy found sticks in the sandpile, so he scratched out an *S* five times. Sammy had a very constructive, happy day at school. Name writing was imbedded in almost everything he did. He saw, read, or wrote his name more than ten times. He was happily learning a lot about written language.

My classroom was full of appropriate writing experiences. I taught my aides, volunteers, students, and colleagues how to provide a rich literacy environment and how to encourage writing by responding appropriately to children's attempts at early writing. I documented each child's progress as he or she moved through the sequence to be used in progress charts. I used the words of the developmental writing sequence to explain to parents what their children knew about writing, what they could expect next, and how to encourage writing at home. I got so I could glance at children's name writing and know exactly what to say to help them expand their understanding of written language.

Most of the children in my classes could write their name (it might still be in all capitals) before they went to kindergarten, even though they had never had a lesson in staying on the line, been told to hold their pencil correctly, asked to copy or trace their names, or been criticized for less than perfect penmanship. Instead, they gradually learned to write their names. They knew a lot about written language, and they loved to write. They had gone from scribbles to name writing.

Share Your Reflections with Evelyn

Write a letter to Evelyn at ELiebermanReflect@gmail.com with your reflections on how she was learning to negotiate the curriculum to respect the children's themes as well as help them learn the academic content that would benefit them in school. Consider including your thoughts about the following:

- What examples did you read of Evelyn's excitement about being a teacher-researcher?

- What specific steps did she take to learn more about the children's understandings of literacy and writing?

- How did she negotiate the curriculum to extend the children's thinking and understandings about early literacy?

- How did Evelyn involve and inform the children's families in her work?

 Practice What You've Learned

Notes about Your Current Approach to Teaching Academics

What specific routines in your current classroom culture promote wonder, curiosity, and learning about learning?

_____

_____

_____

_____

_____

Where could you introduce more specific attention to giving children vocabulary for scientific inquiry or academic learning domains?

_____

_____

_____

_____

_____

_____

_____

_____

How will you strengthen your own knowledge of children's learning in a particular academic area?

_____

_____

_____

_____

_____

_____

_____

_____

Caring for Infants and Toddlers

 Beginning Reflections

Which of the following is the primary way you think about infants and toddlers?

- Babies are so cute and have such adorable antics. They deserve adults who delight in them.

- Babies are fragile and unable to care for themselves. They need constant care and attention.

- Babies get into everything. They need adults to keep them safe.

- Babies are active explorers and natural scientists. They deserve opportunity for rich learning experiences.

Although all of the above statements about babies are true, it's useful for you, as an infant and toddler teacher to reflect on your predominate view of the children you spend your days with. How you think about your babies and their ways in the world will determine how you plan for and respond to them. Use the space on the following page to jot down how you view infants and toddlers.

_____

_____

_____

_____

_____

_____

Use the ideas and activities in this chapter to expand your view and see the opportunity you have to observe and experience one of the most amazing and rapid periods of human development.

What's the Curriculum?

Today infant educators Helen and Miss Sherrial find a rare minute to sit and talk. Baby Ruby sucks on a toy, watching Miss Sherrial fold diapers on the floor beside her. In the rocking chair, Helen gives Louis his bottle. The other babies are all asleep. "Our curriculum plans are due again tomorrow, aren't they?" sighs Helen. "What shall we do? It's April. Maybe we should cut out umbrellas and raindrops to put on the wall." "Whatever," responds Miss Sherrial. "I always feel stupid trying to make up curriculum plans for babies."

Noticing Miss Sherrial's disgruntled expression, Ruby begins kicking her feet, frowning, and making sounds. "Look at you, Ruby; you've got something to say about this too. Here, come sit with Miss Sherrial and tell us what your curriculum should be."

Caregivers who have school on their mind may find that planning a curriculum for infants and toddlers is a challenge. _Curriculum_ is a school word, as is the label _teacher_. What you call yourself and your view of curriculum has a big impact on how you see your role with babies. Some of the most significant learning happens during the caretaking tasks and other opportunities for exploration in your program. As a teacher, caregiver, or educator, if you are thinking about your work and observing children closely, you probably think like Miss Sherrial, the teacher in the scenario, does. What do April umbrellas mean to an infant or valentines and shamrocks to a toddler? The teachers in the scenario are right—these are school themes. Yet these themes are often the only framework teachers have for dutifully trying to meet requirements for curriculum plans. Although she might not realize it, Miss Sherrial has the right idea. Interactive responses to cues from the children are the first element in curriculum for toddlers and infants.

Read the scenario again. Notice Baby Ruby's amazing ability to follow and make meaning of what her teacher is doing. When she sees Miss Sherrial's face and hears a different tone in her voice, Ruby becomes worried. She communicates this with the language of her body and voice. Miss Sherrial lets Ruby know her message was received and responds with some comforting lap time.

Educators who work with infants and toddlers have the opportunity to observe and experience one of the most amazing and rapid periods of human development. It is a time when children are most acutely learning who they are and about the wondrous world they live in. The adults and their interactions and responses to the children and the environment and materials they provide have a profound impact on these babies.

As J. Ronald Lally (1995), codirector of the Program for Infant/ Toddler Care (PITC) of WestEd in California, describes it, "in infant and toddler caregiving, more is happening than tender loving care and learning games—values and beliefs are being witnessed and incorporated. The way you act is perceived, interpreted, and incorporated into the actual definition of the self the child is forming" (Lally 1995, 59).

Relationships Are the Curriculum

For infants and toddlers, responsive interactions are central to what curriculum is about. Usually we don't think about responding to babies as a "plan"; we do it at a subconscious level. We act—and react—to a child's body movement, facial expression, and a certain cry or giggle. We change a wet diaper, feed a hungry belly, and offer a toy to capture a baby's interest. Often we do all of this without a second thought, without noticing the complexity of what is involved in these brief, ordinary exchanges. But when you look closely at what is happening and its significance, the ordinary becomes extraordinary.

In the caregiving relationship, infants and toddlers are learning who they are and what they are capable of in each of these small moments with adults. The children are subconsciously searching for answers to questions such as the following:

- Is the world a safe place?
- Will my needs be met?
- Am I a successful communicator?
- Can I get my message across?
- Will you accept my raw, uncensored emotions?
- How can I learn more about this amazing world?

These are critical issues of trust, which is a primary theme for this stage of development. Other big themes for this time of life include autonomy, separation, and control:

- Can I meet my own needs?
- Do I have any power?
- If we part, will you still be there?

As a teacher of infants and toddlers, your job is to learn about the developmental needs, tasks, and interests of this age group, while coming to know each child's individual way of being and expression. Equally important, you must learn to know yourself so you are conscious of your reactions and can intentionally respond to enhance

the well-being, self-concept, and innate curiosity of each child who depends on you.

The following sections include exercises to help build your awareness and skills for a truly child-centered infant and toddler curriculum.

Use Children's Books

Looking through picture books about infants can remind toddler and infant caregivers of how to think about curriculum for this age group and how to interact with this age group in culturally sensitive ways.

For example, *On the Day I Was Born* by Deborah Chocolate (1995) has illustrations and language that immediately remind the reader of the themes of softness, a sense of belonging, and being the center of attention and the delight of everyone's eye. How can you plan for these themes in your child care program?

Another good example is *Welcoming Babies* by Margy Burns Knight (1994). This book shows the different ways cultural traditions convey a sense of identity and affinity to young children. Examine the elements in this book to enlighten your caregiving practices.

Analyzing books written for toddlers can give you insight into the developmental themes and tasks these children are exploring. Two examples are by Margaret Wise Brown—both of which hold toddlers spellbound.

Goodnight Moon (1947) has simple, clear pictures and text, naming familiar objects over and over again. Children are drawn to the familiarity of the objects and the predictability of the text. This fascination is consistent with their need for safety and trust in their environment and daily routines.

The Runaway Bunny (1942) portrays the intense themes of trust and autonomy as the little bunny asserts her will and independence by climbing mountains and sailing away, only to have her mother assure her that she will always come after her.

The book *Mama, Do You Love Me?* by Barbara Joosse (1991) is a version of the runaway bunny story told within a particular cultural framework. As with Margaret Wise Brown's book, it is also alive with the intense emotions young ones are experiencing—*If I have a big tantrum, even if I'm naughty, will you still love me?*

Be on the lookout for other books that hold children's attention time and time again. As you read through them, ask yourself these questions:

- What do the pictures and colors depict?

- How would I describe the language and rhythm of the text?

- What are the underlying themes of the story?

- How does this book relate to a developmental issue or task of children?

- How can I include these elements in my caregiving environment and routines?

Make Friends with a Baby

Your intuition provides a wealth of understanding about child-centered curriculum for infants and toddlers. Try the following activity with a partner or group of coworkers to help you recognize and name your current knowledge and skills.

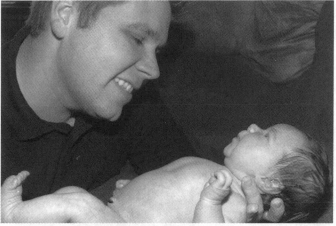

On a sheet of paper, create three columns with the following headings: How do you make friends with a baby? Why does this work? and What does the baby offer in return?

Brainstorm a list of answers for each heading. Be specific. Push yourself to describe more details.

Draw a line under your last entry in each column. Now think about how you can make friends with a toddler, why this works, and what is offered by them. Look over the lists you made to find answers to these questions:

- What are the characteristics and interests of children of this age?

- What are responsive adult roles and interactions for these interests?

- What skills and know-how do infants and toddlers already have?

- How can I use this information to think about curriculum for infants and toddlers?

- What are the sources of interest and reward I find in working with infants and toddlers?

- Can I develop any affirmations from this list to sustain me in my work?

Reading and Responding to Cues

With infants and toddlers, interactions in the caregiving process are primarily based on nonverbal cues. Through our facial expressions and our tone of voice, we adults send and receive hundreds of messages in our daily interactions. These forms of communication, although subtle and at a subconscious level, are extremely powerful. The way we move our bodies, tilt our heads, and touch and hold a child tells that child about herself and the world around her.

Try the following activities to enhance your awareness of the cues you read and send in working with infants and toddlers.

Analyze Pictures

Gather a collection of photographs from magazines, newspapers, and books of infants and toddlers doing various activities. Practice reading cues and analyzing responses by looking at each photo and asking yourself the following questions:

- How does this picture make me feel?

- What do I think this child needs?

- What is this child curious about or trying to figure out?

- How do I know this?

- What would my response and specific behavior be with this child?

How do you think the child in the photograph would perceive your responses? Consider these questions from the child's perspective:

- How successful are my messages to this person?

- How interesting am I?

- Are my feelings understood and acceptable?

- Is it safe to be myself?

- What should I fear?

- Is it okay to investigate this?

Observe Interactions between Adults and Children

In a store, restaurant, or shopping mall, observe an adult and an infant or toddler for about five minutes. Use the questions above to analyze your observations of their interactions.

After practicing with photos and other children and adults, use the same questions to analyze an interaction of your own with a toddler or infant in your care.

Principles for Reading and Responding to Children's Cues

As you continue to develop your ability to read and respond to infant and toddler cues, keep the following points in mind.

Observe. What nonverbal message is the child sending? From the child's point of view, what is he trying to find out or communicate? Consider body language and tone of voice.

Assess. Wait before you respond. Try to determine what is influencing your feelings about what the child is doing. Look at your own body language to assess what it is communicating. Is your message a useful one for the child?

Accept. Whether or not you agree with or like what the child is doing or communicating, use body language to acknowledge you understand what she is trying to do or tell you.

Support. Help the child meet his needs or interests or accomplish what he is trying to do in a safe, acceptable manner.

Everyday Caregiving Routines Are a Source of Curriculum

The caregiving process is central to infant and toddler curriculum because it fosters a child's development and positive identity. The more you increase your awareness that everyday materials, activities, and routines constitute a curriculum, the more you will value this idea and help others to see it.

Use the following activity to practice recognizing and describing how everyday actions are important.

Analyze Caregiving Routines

Gather several catalogs with materials and equipment that support caregiving activities with infants and toddlers or look more closely at your own environment. On a sheet of paper, make five columns with the following headings: Caregiving Routines; What Happens Here?; Social/ Emotional Learning; Language/Cognitive Learning; Sensory/Motor Learning.

Write the name of the object or equipment under the Caregiving Routines column. Then fill in answers under each of the remaining columns. As an example, look through the following chart and add more of your ideas.

Caretaking Routines	What Happens Here?	Social/ Emotional Learning	Language/ Cognitive Learning	Sensory/ Motor Learning
Toddler diaper changing station with steps.	Teacher responds to child's need for diaper change.	Trust is reinforced because adult helps meet child's need.	Child hears vocabulary.	Teacher helps child notice the difference between wet and dry.
	Teacher talks about wet diaper.	Child's sense of self-worth grows from atten-tion and warm response.	Child connects language to experience.	Child uses arms and hands to pull up pants.
	Teacher uses warm voice, smile, and gentle touch.	Child experi-ences warm conversation and relationship.	Child connects experience to mental images.	Child practices climbing stairs.
	Teacher describes what she is doing as she changes diaper.	Child's autonomy grows with involvement in process.	Child explores cause and effect.	
	Teacher responds to child's interest.	Child feels valued and capable.		
	Teacher helps child feel dry diaper.			
	Teacher offers child role in pull-ing up pants.			
	Teacher helps child walk up and down stairs to diaper station.			

Nurture Lively Minds

In recent years, both in the media and throughout the early childhood profession, a great deal of attention has been given to the importance of brain development in infants and toddlers. Yet the learning that infants and toddlers are pursuing at this stage of development is filled with small, discrete elements that adults acquired long ago, so we don't easily recognize or remember them. It's easy to dismiss infants' and toddlers' explorations of the world around them because they move quickly, make messes, and put themselves in seemingly risky situations. Seeing the significance of what babies are learning requires that teachers develop the practice of waiting before jumping into a situation. You need to notice the small details and determine what the thinking going on underneath a child's behavior might be. When you do this, you will come to see that with most everything they do, even the youngest babies have something in mind. Whether or not they are conscious of it, they have a purpose or question they are pursuing. When you take even their smallest actions seriously, you will be astonished by children's deep engagement with the simple wonders around them.

It takes daily practice for teachers to really see babies' learning pursuits. Try the following activities to help you enhance your ability to respond to and enhance learning moments with infants and toddlers.

Study Photos of Infants and Toddlers

Take photos of the infants and toddlers you work with, making sure you focus on close-up shots of their interactions or relationship to a material or another person. Use your computer or camera photo program to crop all the external scenery and enlarge the image of the child interacting with materials and others. Now you have a good photo to study.

Practice the following with each photo:

- Notice the details in the photo, including the child's body language and facial expressions—what he is looking at, touching, moving, etc.

- To see her point of view, try to put yourself in the child's shoes. What can you say about the child's perspectives, interests, curiosity in the photo?

- What small elements in his intention or actions could help you identify what the child may be learning?

- What are you drawn to in the photo? What interests, curiosities, surprises, and delights do you feel when you look at what the child is doing in the photo?

- Create a list of words to describe the details of what you see in the photo.

The photos will show you how children bring their whole selves—body, mind, and emotions—to every task.

Offer Engaging Activities

When you examine the typical toys designed for infants and toddlers, you come to see how limited they are for engaging the lively minds of these amazing people. The typical materials are bright, primary-colored, hard plastic surfaces with commercial cartoon figures that are meant to capture children's attention or entertain them. They usually have a cause-and-effect component that the child stumbles upon or is shown, typically a button or knob that rings a bell, whistles, beeps, or lights up when you push it. Once the child figures out the simple command for using the toy, there is little else to engage with.

What do these materials say about how young children learn? Inherent in these toys is the view that infants and toddlers have limited capabilities or inner resources, that they require attention-grabbing, over-stimulating external experiences to stay interested in something. These materials do little to engage children's extraordinary sensory capabilities or lively minds, tap into their deep desire to learn, hone their skills and abilities, or cultivate sustained attention to their explorations.

You can find more engaging and unusual materials at garage sales and thrift stores and then offer them in careful combination and collections. You can help the children focus if you set the materials out in an engaging way on a particular rug signifying a special time for exploration, or bring a bag or box to the rug and invite the children to slowly empty the contents and examine all the interesting objects inside. See our book *Learning Together with Young Children* (2008) for more guidance on this idea of how to offer materials.

Here is a list of a few engaging collections for exploration.

Massage Tools

Collect from thrift shops numerous shapes and sizes of these wooden treasures. Their lovely natural wood color and texture with various grooves and indents make them intriguing to look at, touch, and study. The most interesting aspects of them are their wheels and other moving parts.

Fur and Fabric

Offer interesting animal prints or a variety of faux fur pieces and fabrics that are soft, shaggy, and of different colors and textures. Offer these as a collection with stuffed animals that match the prints and fur pieces. Include some brushes for the children to use on the fur.

Tubes and Balls

Collect a variety of clear plastic and hard cardboard tubes of varying widths and lengths. Along with these provide numerous kinds of balls, small and large: craft balls, cotton balls, Wiffle balls, table-tennis balls, golf balls, tennis balls, and balls with rolling eyes. Add to these a collection of lengths of rope as another item for the children to push through the tubes.

Natural Items

Gather a variety of seashells, pinecones, rocks, gourds, and pods, along with boxes and baskets for sorting and hiding.

Coaster Sets and Napkin Rings

These make wonderful "toys" for exploration and manipulation. Coasters come in all shapes and sizes, often with matching boxes that they fit in. Napkin rings are great for stacking and rolling as well as for stringing when offered with lengths of ribbon.

Light and Color Explorations

Offer an array of flashlights, color paddles, prisms, and other colorful translucent objects that the children can use to look through, build with, or make colorful shadow patterns with. If possible, alternately offer these with a small light table, an overhead projector, or with flashlights, and then turn the overhead lights off.

Observe Children Exploring Interesting Materials

As they play with the materials, observe to see whether the children are pursuing any of the following questions:

Exploration of Sensory Elements

- What does this look like?
- What does this feel like?
- What does this sound like?
- What does this smell like?
- What does this taste like?

Exploration of Function and Relationship

- How does this move?
- What can this do?
- What can I do with this?
- How do these things work together?
- How can I use this to connect with others?
- What can this be?
- How can I use this in a game or drama?

What did you discover? During your observation, did you think of other materials you might look for? Finding interesting materials for the children can began to feel like a hunt for treasures and gifts to offer them. As you look for more engaging materials, use these questions as your guide:

- Will the children be drawn to the textures, shapes, and colors of particular collections of materials?
- Will they enjoy manipulating the various props for investigation and discovery?

- Will the materials help them focus, use purposeful actions, and stay with an investigation for long periods of time?

- Will the materials support the children's explorations of ideas and theories and fuel their intense passion to learn?

Responding to Enhance Explorations

When you study photos of babies and observe them exploring interesting materials, you capture the significance of their investigations. Rather than responding to children with quick judgments and reactions, you are motivated to find the moments that capture your heart and mind and offer them more engaging activities to do. As they work, you respond to enhance their explorations.

What you give attention to, in turn, supports the children's attention and communicates that their pursuits have value. When you offer them engaging activities to capture their lively minds and share new words and phrases to describe what you see them doing and thinking, you help them build vocabulary as well as attach their experiences to mental images.

When you study children's actions for their larger significance, you become intellectually engaged side by side with the children in their pursuits and you see more clearly their lively minds at work and respond in ways that enhance their identity as serious thinkers and learners.

Stop next time you are with babies as they play. Watch the way they immerse themselves in the rich and magical world around them. Notice the great skill they bring to exploration and discovery. Share in their joy of being alert and alive. You will witness complex learning at work for the children, and if you open yourself to it, you will learn from them to see the world in new and wondrous ways.

Curriculum Theme Forms

As you become more aware of the curriculum of everyday caregiving as well as come to marvel at the lively minds of the babies you work with, give them the recognition they deserve. Use the following form to plan your curriculum to reflect the meaningful interactions and experiences you have with your infants and toddlers.

Growing Self-Help Curriculum

Environment and materials to promote self-help	Routines and interactions to promote self-help	Observations of efforts children make

Growing Language Curriculum

Environment and materials to promote language	Routines and interactions to promote language	Observations of efforts children make

Growing Brain Curriculum

Environment and materials to promote cognitive development	Routines and interactions to promote cognitive development	Observations of efforts children make

Identity and Self-Esteem Curriculum

Environment and materials to promote identity development and self-esteem	Routines and interactions to promote identity development and self-esteem	Observations of efforts children make

An Inspirational Story

As you read about Deb's return to working with toddlers, notice how even with her decades of experience of working with children and being a teacher-educator, she still recognizes how her thinking is growing about her role. Notice how she uses the metaphor of riding waves in her first story, and how this expands her looking back years later. Consider what metaphor might guide your work with toddlers.

Riding the Waves Again:
About Returning to Work with Toddlers

Deb Curtis, Toddler Teacher

I am working with two-year-olds again. I haven't had this kind of daily responsibility or relationships with a group of children for about fifteen years. I have a lot of knowledge and understanding of their development and also lots of strategies for working with a group of children, all of which I have deeply constructed through my years of teacher training. It's wonderful to be able to stop and think about what's going on and wait awhile to see what happens. As the weeks go by, my relationships with individual children are forming as I begin to know each of them for who they are. They seem to like me too! And I think I'm getting quite good again at being with them.

I'm also a bit cautious and clumsy at times. What I am still in the process of relearning is the intuitive nature of the work. There is a physical and emotional rhythm that the group seems to have—at times the children are so engaged and cohesive that the room almost hums with a steady, melodic beat. Then there are moments when it changes to a cacophony of sounds and bodies, all colliding as they move in their individual rhythms. There's not really a way to control it; you can only watch closely and respond accordingly. You have to anticipate what might happen, try to stay one step ahead of them, and follow their lead as events unfold. And you have to do this while staying focused with them in the moment.

It reminds me of learning to swim in the ocean. You only master an understanding of the nature of waves by spending quite a bit of time with your body immersed in the experience. You have to be able to anticipate what's going to happen and follow the lead of the waves, but at the same time remain totally observant and aware of what's happening with all the elements at each moment. You can never really be in control or change the waves. You just learn to understand how to respond to them. You know when to go over the top, because you've missed your opportunity to catch the wave. You learn when to dive under, because if you don't, the wave will crash on you and send you whirling and twirling with it to the shore. But when that happens, you quickly realize that you should just relax and go with it. You also know when you've caught the wave just at the optimum moment to ride smoothly on the crest and land gently in a pool at the bottom. If you try to fight against the waves rather than learning to respond in these ways, your experience of the ocean is scary and exhausting.

This really does describe the way I've been experiencing relearning to work with a group of two-year-olds. It's not that I don't take charge when I need to. I was worried that I wouldn't know how to do that again. I quickly remembered how because I was immediately involved in situations where I had to. I guess this thing I'm trying to describe is the part of teaching that isn't about planning or leading, but about learning to stay with the process.

2010 Postscript: Looking Back, Looking Forward

I've spent quite a few more years working directly with toddlers, and I still believe what I wrote fourteen years ago is the foundation for the role I play with them today. Toddlers live in the moment, experiencing the joys and challenges of their lives with full emotion and expression. I have learned so much from them about embracing and immersing myself in ordinary moments, as they've helped me cultivate patience and flexibility.

Understanding the rhythm of toddlers is being able to go with the flow and stay with the process, riding the waves. Not fighting or trying to change the nature of toddlers is critical to the work. I can't control toddlers, nor do I want to. I have come to realize that my view of my role back then was less active than I see my work now.

Rather than just understanding the waves and how to negotiate while in them, I have expanded the wave metaphor. Now I see myself more as the surfer, using my understandings and skills to utilize the full potential of the wave. A surfer knows the waves well. She sees their power, respects their natural ways, and knows she can't control them. But she also has cultivated her skills in catching and riding them. She knows how to use her balance to get up and stay up. She knows how to use the board to stay at the top of a wave or find just the right place in the tube to capture the speed and go the distance. The surfer's role is an active one, for she is constantly observing the ever-changing nature of the waves and adjusting her attention and actions to work with what unfolds or to move on and find the next wave she wants to ride. The wave is not in charge, and neither is the surfer. It is truly a cooperative venture.

And so it is with my work with toddlers. I take a lot more initiative now to offer my ideas to help build on their ideas and actions. I don't just wait for them to speed in with their big energy. I plan for their eager ways in the world, offering interesting activities and materials to invite explorations. I notice their interactions and words with each other and offer them back in new ways that expand their play skills, friendships, and collaboration with each other. I've come to see their power and competence. I respect their abilities and potential and believe that they will benefit from my coaching. We work side by side, bringing our ideas, skills, and passions; we coconstruct meaning and learn together. This, too, is a cooperative venture!

Share Your Reflections with Deb

Write a letter to Deb at DCurtisReflect@gmail.com with your reflections on how she was learning to negotiate the curriculum to respect her toddlers' ways in the world. Consider including your thoughts about the following:

- What did she learn about herself in the initial story and in her reflections a decade later?

- What new insights did she learn about the children's perspectives?

- How would you describe Deb's view of the toddlers she works with?

- How did her view of the role of the teacher change in her work with toddlers?

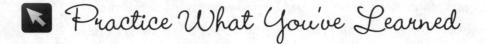

Practice What You've Learned

Notes about Your Current Approach to Caring for Infants and Toddlers

Use this space to reflect on your approach to caring for infants and toddlers. The following questions will get you started.

How can you become more aware of your nonverbal cues to infants and toddlers?

_____

_____

_____

_____

What everyday routines could you turn into a curriculum chart for recording your observations?

_____

_____

_____

_____

What new materials will you offer to engage infants' and toddlers' lively minds?

_____

_____

_____

_____

_____

What will you do to notice and enhance infants' and toddlers' curiosity and learning?

_____

_____

_____

_____

_____

What other changes would you like to make?

_____

_____

_____

_____

_____

_____

Organizing, Evaluating, and Communicating Your Approach

8

▶ Beginning Reflections

If someone were to ask you to describe child-centered curriculum, what would you say?

Write your initial thoughts in the space below.

_____

_____

_____

_____

_____

_____

_____

_____

_____

Your director requires you to turn in your curriculum plans for each of the coming months. However, you want to use a child-centered emergent approach, basing your plans on observations of themes in the children's lives and their play. The licensor reminds you that your state's new early learning standards call for a research-based curriculum. How can you meet the state's requirements using a child-centered emergent approach? Wanting to build your curriculum around the children's themes, you have been carefully observing and listening. So far, no obvious theme has emerged. The children are primarily talking about Batman and Barbie, and you want to discourage, not emphasize, that interest. What should you do? A parent comes to you with a newspaper article on a federal report saying that children are coming to school unprepared and that preschools must get more rigorous in teaching academics. You know that a child-centered, play-based curriculum can work, but everything—and everyone—seems to be working against you. How can you convince that parent of your approach?

The approach to child-centered curriculum advocated in this book often seems hampered by the requirements for research-based curricula and the academic expectations of supervisors and parents. There is a great deal of misinformation and blaming about the roots of school failure.

Nevertheless, one fact remains clear: A child-centered, culturally relevant curriculum approach is grounded in solid theories and research about the teaching and learning process and the identity development of young children. When offered as an intentional, thoughtful practice, this approach to teaching engages children's competencies, their eagerness to learn and form relationships, *and* addresses standards. Your challenge as a child-centered teacher is to get organized and then articulate to parents and others what you are doing and why. Then continue to study how theories translate to practice and how your practice can inform the theory.

Where Do You Begin?

Many teachers have trouble figuring out how to start using a child-centered curriculum approach. At first, the idea of following the children's lead creates visions of chaos and confusion. Here are some typical teacher responses:

"How can I just let the children do what they want?"

"What will the parents say?"

"The children won't learn anything!"

On the surface, using a child-centered approach may sound as though the teacher has no goals or objectives for the children. You might picture the teacher just sitting around waiting for something to emerge from the children. Nothing could be further from the truth. When you really investigate the pedagogical theories underpinning the approach this book advocates, you come to understand that a child-centered curriculum requires a much more complex view of teaching and learning than a traditional one. A child-centered emergent approach has as much structure as a teacher-directed approach. With an emergent approach, the source of the structure is the teacher's belief that children are capable of deep engagement with things that interest them. They deserve to have curriculum built on this rather than following an activity book or teacher script. The teacher creates a well-planned environment with engaging materials and establishes a classroom culture of excitement about learning. To plan ways to meet standards and early learning guidelines, she draws on her observations of how the children are engaging in activities. Intentional teachers take children's ideas seriously and use them to craft their curriculum plans.

Cocreating the Curriculum

For most teachers, learning to use a child-centered emergent curriculum approach is a developmental process. It takes time to

- **Shift** your view of what curriculum really is;

- **Build** collaborative relationships with children, their families, and your coworkers;

- **Design** and maintain a carefully planned environment;

- **Establish** a classroom culture where children self-regulate, care for each other and the materials, and help establish daily routines, rituals, and special celebrations;

- **Develop** advanced skills in observing children;

- **Learn** to analyze children's thinking and development to see new levels of complexity and connections to discrete elements of the learning domains;

- **Practice** new skills and try out ideas; and

- **Experience** excitement that leads to trusting the children and oneself—and the curriculum that is being cocreated.

The following descriptions of thematic approaches to emergent curriculum, as well as the stories at the end of each chapter in this handbook, reflect various approaches to child-centered curriculum that family providers and teachers have adopted. Some of these professionals have made small but significant changes in the face of pressures for academic lessons and preparing for high-stakes tests. Others have moved to complex levels of understanding and sophistication in their planning, assessing, and responding to children's interests and needs.

Start where you are comfortable. Maybe you can set aside a specific time of day to focus on the children's interests. While introducing a traditional curriculum theme or proscribed curriculum, you may recognize children are pursuing their own questions, and you may decide to abandon yours in favor of theirs. Perhaps you'll come to integrate a responsive child-centered approach throughout your daily routine. Once you begin to work with the children to develop curriculum in this way, your time together will flourish. You'll find a new meaning in the idea of curriculum themes and projects.

Thematic Approaches to Child-Centered Curriculum

Before you read any further, look back at your self-reflections and assessments in the first seven chapters of this handbook. Then consider which of the following approaches to child-centered curriculum represents your current thinking or teaching practices. Are you satisfied with what you are doing, or would you like to develop one of the other approaches described?

You might also want to return to these descriptions after you have read all of the teacher stories at the end of each chapter. Continually assess where you are and cultivate a vision of where you would like to be in your approach to curriculum planning. From time to time ask yourself the following questions:

- Are there understandings that are still not clear to me?

- Would some further study or additional skills be helpful?

- Who could I use as a role model and mentor?

- Who might I help by being a mentor and role model?

Based on your responses to these questions, make a plan to continue your professional development. You could seek out resources on the Internet, become involved in professional organizations in your community, or visit programs with a known philosophy that values play and curriculum that is responsive to children.

Topical Themes

A teacher or family provider using the topical themes approach has made a small but significant change in how he views curriculum planning. While he may still use a traditional theme-based approach, the themes he plans come from the emerging interests and events in the children's lives throughout the year, rather than from a preplanned schedule for the year.

For example, the hometown baseball team might be in the World Series and all of the children and their families are wrapped up in the excitement. The teacher uses a baseball theme to plan activities, projects, and field trips.

Environmental Themes

Observing how the children are using materials in various areas of the room, a family provider or teacher using environmental themes regularly adds more materials and activities to enhance her involvement and provide for further exploration.

For example, the teacher notices that the block area is overflowing with children building creations. She adds a variety of different kinds of blocks, building materials, pictures of construction sites, and related props in other parts of the room, such as the art and dress-up areas.

Developmental Themes

Learning more about such things as sensory motor development and the stages of play, the teacher observes the developmental tasks that children are practicing. He then provides more interactions, activities, and materials to scaffold the learning process.

For example, the caregiver notices that many of the older babies in his group are pulling themselves up and finding support for learning to walk. He provides structures (e.g., furniture and cushions) for the babies to pull themselves up and hold on to while standing. He also adds sturdy wheeled toys to push and practice walking.

Project Themes

The teacher who uses project themes follows the children's ideas and interests as they play, providing materials and activities that pick up on and extend the various themes they are pursuing.

For example, when doll play in the dress-up area begins to include taking care of a sick baby, the teacher adds props for doctor and medical play that sustains this play. Later, to extend this theme, she provides boxes, wheels, and paint in the art area for children to create ambulances and aid cars. They take field trips to medical clinics and hospitals or invite nurses, doctors, and EMTs to talk to the children.

In-Depth Study Themes

This approach involves a complex form of curriculum in which teachers closely observe and analyze children's thinking and actions around a topic of interest. The teachers then provide numerous avenues for the children to explore and construct their understandings around the theme. Teachers in the schools of Reggio Emilia refer to this as providing for "the hundred languages of children." Teachers facilitate children's long-term involvement in the exploration process and development of thought. As teachers hypothesize about the significance of what children are pursuing and provide further opportunities to explore, the project becomes an arena for many developmental themes and also for meeting standards. Teachers and children are cocreators of the curriculum, and in-depth studies often last for months. The teacher stories at the end of chapters 4 and 5 describe the complexity involved in this approach to sustaining an in-depth study. You will find more ideas in our book *Learning Together with Young Children* (2008) and in numerous books on Reggio-inspired practices.

As you develop your personal approach to a child-centered emergent curriculum, find a planning process that works for you. This involves developing a way to focus your thinking and to generate ideas about possible directions for the curriculum. Then create a method for documenting what actually happens—where the children take the curriculum, how hypotheses get tested, and when ideas begin to take hold. Consider strategies to connect the unfolding events with academic content and early learning guidelines.

Getting Organized

As you build your curriculum on children's interests and developmental themes, you'll need to develop the following as a foundation for this work:

- a well-planned, visually pleasing, and inviting learning environment for your classroom

- a basic schedule and set of routines that provide security and flexibility for children

- a guiding framework for decision making about themes to pursue

- an understanding of your new roles, dispositions, and skills for interactions and interventions with children

The Learning Environment and Routines

As stated earlier, one source of a structure underpinning a child-centered emergent approach is the teacher's belief that children are capable of deep engagement with things that interest them. This is foundational to the success of this approach, along with two other areas—the learning environment and routines. Without careful, ongoing attention to creating an engaging learning environment, teachers risk subjecting children to boredom, restlessness, and the attending behaviors this provokes in children. When teachers use a child-centered emergent approach to curriculum, they are continually planning and adjusting the environment and materials they offer children. Likewise, teachers give careful attention to engaging the children in setting up daily routines

that foster children's self-regulation and identity of being a member of an exciting learning community. You can find extensive ideas on these two foundational elements in our books *Designs for Living and Learning* (2003) and *Learning Together with Young Children* (2008). The following are key points to keep in mind.

- Provide a well-organized, aesthetically pleasing environment with materials that stimulate the senses, engage curiosity, and invite inquiry.

- Structure large blocks of time for investigation and play.

- Create a space that can be used for a group of children to pursue an ongoing project or in-depth study.

- Surround the children with representations of their lives, home, and classroom community.

A Framework for Deciding on Curriculum to Pursue

If you closely attend to children's play and conversations, each day you will uncover possible themes to pursue in your curriculum planning. To avoid bouncing around and losing focus, it's helpful to have the following as a framework to guide your decision making.

- Identify underlying themes that could evolve into a project or investigation.

- Choose projects that reflect your values and engage your curiosity as well as the children's.

- Pursue themes that are readily observable to children and engage their perspectives.

- Develop activities that generate complexity and relationships from one day to the next.

- Offer many possible ways to investigate, represent, and revisit ideas being explored.

Teacher Roles and Skills to Acquire

Many educators think of teaching as a process of telling or instructing the children. But teaching with a child-centered approach requires some new ways of thinking and acting as a teacher. You ask yourself more questions than you ask the children. You engage in a cycle of planning that involves knowing yourself well, along with keen awareness of the children and the goals you have for them. You continually strive to strengthen your relationships with your coworkers and the children's families.

- Know yourself, your passions, values, and hot buttons.
- Listen, observe, document, and analyze.
- Seek other perspectives from colleagues and the children's families.
- Initiate projects with an invitation or "provocation" to capture the children's attention.
- Build on the children's perspectives, questions, and pursuits.
- Study the language and concepts of the learning domains (science, math, literacy) and how to support these as part of children's learning through their self-initiated activities and interests.
- Document the learning process inside the project.
- Use your documentation to help children revisit and extend their ideas, questions, and interests.
- Use your documentation to help you analyze and assess whether your curriculum is engaging children in complex ideas that lead to desired outcomes.

The Planning Process

Curriculum comes from many places—observations of children's interests, their families, experiences, community, and seasonal events. It can come from your life as a teacher as well—a passion, hobby, or particular event that has influenced you.

Curriculum may get introduced by something that unfolds in the life of your classroom community or by a provocation you as the teacher offer—something for the children to discover, uncover, investigate, or experiment with. Once the process happens, your primary job is to observe. Directing questions to yourself, rather than to children, will help you follow their lead and offer the resources and support they need. Your own analysis will help you assess whether your decisions are leading to an engaging curriculum. Here are some questions to guide your observations as curriculum is emerging:

- What do the children find interesting about this?
- What do they already seem to know, accurately or with misconceptions?
- What are their questions?
- How could they represent their understandings?
- What learning domains are reflected in their play?

A Four-Step Planning Process

The following four steps can serve as a framework for planning a child-centered curriculum.

Step 1: Provision the Environment

Provide enough materials and space for children to explore. What props would help children explore a given theme? How could you arrange these as an invitation or provocation? Consider props for the dress-up, block, art, and table areas. For example, if the theme seems to be "Caring for Babies," you might provide baby dolls, blankets, and beds. Creating a provocation or sparking an interest might mean a visit from a newborn baby or a pregnant mother or a recording of a crying baby placed in the home center.

As the children become involved with the initial materials, careful observation will assist you in planning your next steps. Use the following questions to gain more information:

- What are the children doing with what is provided?

- What about the materials seems fun and pleasurable to the children? What materials are not being used as much? Why not?

- What themes do they talk about and represent?

- What experiences, people, and objects are in their play?

- What are the children inventing, questioning, or understanding?

- What underlying or development themes do I think might be at the center of this interest for the children?

- What learning domains are present in their play?

Step 2: Sustain the Play

Once children are absorbed in a play theme, you can do several things to sustain the activity. For example, with the "Caring for Babies" theme, you can provide more props—a bottle, high chair, car seat, bathing tub, stroller, sling, backpack carrier, and an array of photographs. Include images of the children, their family members, and yourself as babies. At this point, try to limit your involvement to asking open-ended questions, making leading statements, helping problem solve, and providing conflict resolution when necessary to keep the play going.

Observe again during this sustained play and ask yourself the following questions for cues to enrich the play theme and the children's learning:

- What other materials might the children use to extend their experience or represent their ideas and feelings?

- What additional activities might be relevant and offer a way to integrate academic learning or state standards?

- How are children building from one day's experience to the next?

- What new ideas, solutions, or answers are the children coming up with? Is there a way to build on these ideas to deepen or challenge children's thinking?

Step 3: Enrich the Play

If you notice interest waning or the children needing more complexity to sustain their involvement, enrich the project with props that might help spark new ideas. Questions to ask yourself at this point include the following:

- What could I offer that would connect this play to the children's family life?

- Are their cultural variations related to this theme that we could explore?

- Where might we visit or who in the community might we involve?

- How could we offer more complexity to challenge the children to go deeper?

For instance, in the "Caring for Babies" play, you might do the following:

- Introduce doctor kits or books about the growth and development of babies.

- Add clipboards and pens for the work of caring for babies, e.g., making doctor's appointments, writing prescriptions.

- Add scales and measuring tape for recording growth, e.g., weighing and measuring, creating growth charts.

- Create matching games with the children's baby pictures and current ones.

- Have a visit from a real baby or take a field trip to places that serve or care for babies.

- Explore where babies come from and how they grow and come into the world.

- Include examples of different kinds of animal babies, perhaps leading to classifications of how babies are born in different animal families—mammals, birds, reptiles, and so forth.

Step 4: Represent and Rerepresent the Experience

Representation, or using symbols to represent ideas, is the foundation for broader language and literacy development. An important step in the process of moving children to a deeper level of thinking is to provide them with opportunities to represent their understandings with

different materials—"the hundred languages" approach used in the schools of Reggio Emilia. Rerepresenting their ideas in a new or different way provides children opportunities to expand their symbolic thinking, creative expression, and visual literacy. New representations of their play and thinking might involve drawing, painting, sculpting, creating with recycled loose parts, storytelling, or dramatic play. Your choice of materials depends on the focus of the children and the ideas you come up with to keep them engaged in a meaningful way.

If you develop a routine of regularly having children draw an idea they have, or perhaps something they have been building in the block area, they will often begin to initiate this representational work themselves. You can provoke further thinking by asking about something that piques your curiosity, suggesting they work together with a friend, or combining all their drawings into one representation. With the "Caring for Babies" theme, you could try things like the following:

- Suggest they dictate and illustrate a story about the ways that families care for babies.

- Invite the children to draw different ways to feed babies. Provoke their thinking about food that doesn't require teeth for chewing and about different cultural practices.

- Offer clay for the children to represent foods for babies or to represent human or animal babies at different ages.

- Suggest the children study pictures of the different ways babies are carried in different cultures and ask them to create props and act this out.

Documenting How Curriculum Unfolds

Documentation has become a big focus in early childhood education. As a home provider or teacher, working on documentation can either become just another meaningless task or requirement, or it can be one of the most useful processes you have for developing meaningful child-centered curriculum. If you see documentation as the way to notice and study what goes on in your work with children, it can be a significant learning tool for you in your work.

Think of documentation first as a process and only secondly as a product. As a process, your documentation can become part of the curriculum activities you do with children. It is your adult work to represent and rerepresent what is happening with the children. For instance:

- Write down children's words and read them back to the children.

- Take photos and caption them together with the children.

- Tell stories together about what the children have been doing.

- Create homemade books about the children's activities.

- Sketch children's creations, such as a block structure, make photocopies, and post one near the block area, or put copies on the art table the next day.

Children love the recognition they get when teachers represent what the children have been doing. It gives further impetus for their own representations. Rerepresenting what they are doing is a powerful tool for children's learning. Experience is not the only teacher. In fact, reflecting on your experience can often lead to your most significant new understandings.

Documentation as a Process

Documenting is a process that helps you think about what is unfolding in your classroom and how to use your observations to create more meaningful curriculum for the children. Here is a diagram to help you visualize how this might work as a way of thinking and working with the documentation process.

You can also draw on our book *The Art of Awareness* (2000) for more ideas to enhance your documenting process.

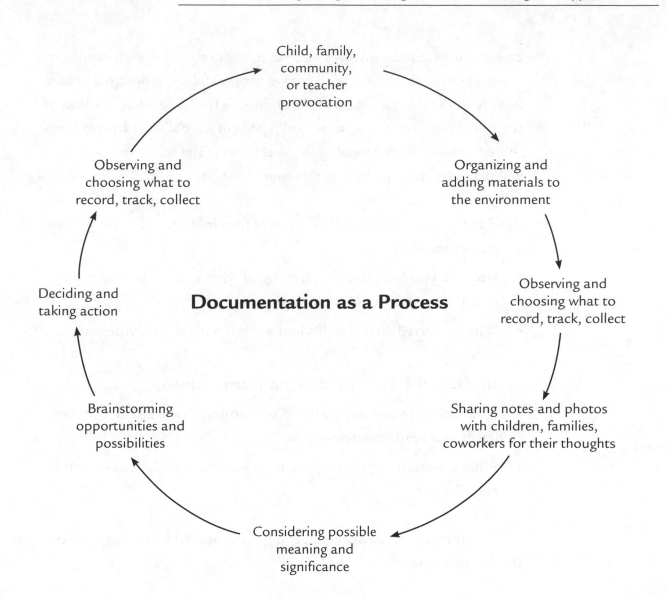

Child, family,
community,
or teacher
provocation

Organizing and
adding materials to
the environment

Observing and
choosing what to
record, track, collect

Documentation as a Process

Observing and
choosing what to
record, track, collect

Deciding and
taking action

Sharing notes and photos
with children, families,
coworkers for their thoughts

Brainstorming
opportunities and
possibilities

Considering possible
meaning and
significance

Documentation as a Product

At different junctures, you will want to cull some of your observation
stories, photos, and samples of children's work to post for others to
read. Some of these will be aimed at adults, while other documentation
can be designed for the children. You may copy things to include in
portfolios or to guide you in completing required assessments. When a
particular piece of documentation demonstrates a wonderful snapshot
of children's competency or tells a story of an in-depth study, you may
want to create a display panel to call people's attention to it. In this

case, documentation involves more than a set of photos with captions. When creating documentation entries for portfolios or posted displays, be sure to include narration of the children's thinking and evolution of their interests, questions, ideas, and representations. You can also learn more from our book *Spreading the News* (1996). The following questions will help you consider how to represent what happened:

- What got this all started? What were the children's beginning ideas and actions?

- How did you interpret the meaning of what was happening, what would be worth pursuing, and why?

- What occurred after the children worked with the activities over time?

- How have the children's ideas and actions changed?

- How can you summarize aspects of learning that relate to the standards and desired outcomes?

- What questions, opportunities, or possibilities could lead to more complexity?

Documentation as a product can be represented by the diagram on the following page.

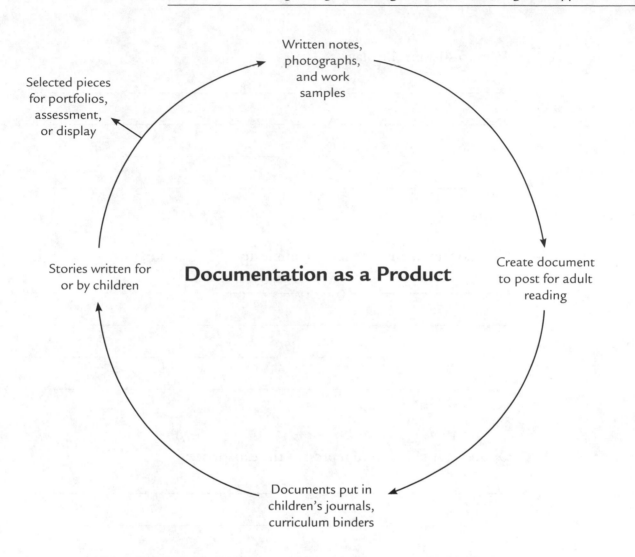

Written notes, photographs, and work samples

Selected pieces for portfolios, assessment, or display

Documentation as a Product

Create document to post for adult reading

Stories written for or by children

Documents put in children's journals, curriculum binders

Practice the Planning Process

Revisit the Four-Step Planning Process described on pages 255–59. Practice this process. Base your plan on this observation: A teacher notices children repeatedly pretending to talk on the phone. As you do this, also return to the Framework for Deciding on page 254.

Initial provision of the environment:

_____

_____

_____

_____

Ways to sustain the play:

_____

_____

_____

_____

Ideas to enrich and add more complexity:

_____

_____

_____

_____

Options for children to represent the experience:

_____

_____

_____

_____

Practice the process again with the following observation: A teacher hears the children's excitement about a fire they saw on the news. Fill in your ideas for enriching and building on the possible themes in this observation.

Initial provision of the environment:

_____

_____

_____

_____

Ways to sustain the play:

_____

_____

_____

_____

Ideas to enrich and add more complexity:

_____

_____

_____

_____

Options for children to represent the experience:

_____

_____

_____

_____

Representing the Curriculum to Others

Most people use elementary, middle, and high school as their frame of reference for planning curriculum. Supervisors, parents, and regulatory agencies expect to see a school-type lesson plan form posted in your room. They think this indicates that you are teaching children what they need to know before entering school.

Because the approach to child-centered curriculum planning advocated in this handbook uses the interests, competencies, questions, and valuable ideas of children, rather than a proscribed curriculum or activity book or a starting point, curriculum plans cannot be confined to little boxes representing times and days of the week. This means you need to reeducate others—parents, administrators, state regulators—about what to expect. They need help to understand how your approach meets the intent of the requirements or expectations they have. You need to be able to articulate a clear understanding of academic learning domains and how they can be folded into your emergent curriculum work.

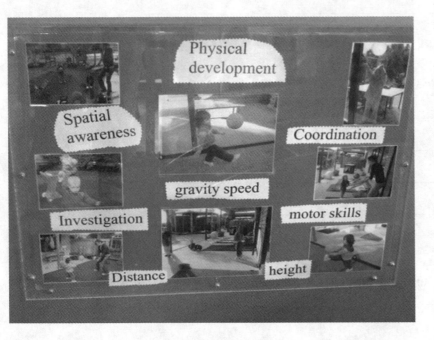

You can use a variety of strategies to describe your planning process or address requirements for written curriculum plans. You'll find here examples you can copy or adapt to meet your specific needs. Experiment with them until you find a format that works for you and satisfies the expectations of others. You will find further examples in our book *Learning Together with Young Children* (2008).

Consider the following examples as a way to post your prethinking about your upcoming curriculum. If you are required to use a preset planning form, translate the ideas of provision–sustain–enrich–represent into the boxes on that form. You can continue to use your prethinking form for yourself to document what actually happens as the curriculum evolves.

Curriculum plans for: _____

Project theme: _____

Initial provision of the environment:

_____
_____
_____
_____
_____

Ways to sustain the play:

_____
_____
_____
_____

Ideas to enrich and add more complexity:

_____
_____
_____
_____
_____

Options for children to represent the experience:

_____
_____
_____
_____
_____

Color-Coded Web

Use a curriculum web format to document the curriculum process as
it emerges. You can use one color to indicate interests and responses
on the part of the children and another color to describe teacher provi-
sions, interventions, enrichments, and so forth. The following web is
an example of a form for documenting the curriculum process as it
emerges.

Example:
Teacher reads *Welcoming Babies*

Provision:
initial materials or play
themes emerged

Enrich:
materials/interactions
expand & add content

Sustain:
materials/interactions
to keep going

Example:
Diane brought pictures of herself as a baby.

Stages-of-Play Web

Plan your environment and activities for any topic or project around the four stages of play. A possible form for this is included here. In creating your own web, start with your starting place, provocation, or topical theme in the center of the page.

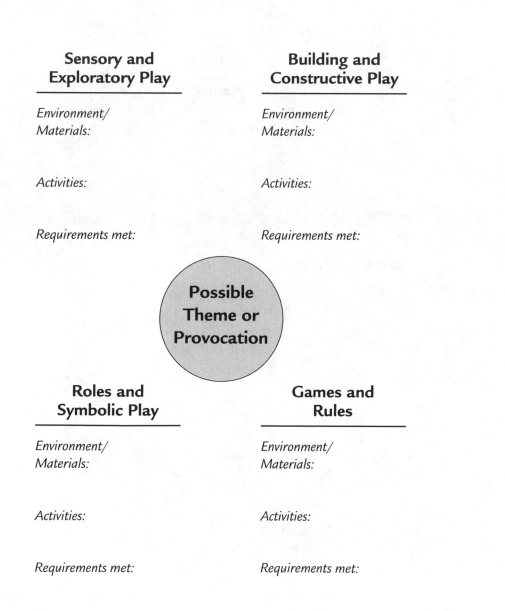

**Sensory and
Exploratory Play**

*Environment/
Materials:*

Activities:

Requirements met:

**Building and
Constructive Play**

*Environment/
Materials:*

Activities:

Requirements met:

**Possible
Theme or
Provocation**

**Roles and
Symbolic Play**

*Environment/
Materials:*

Activities:

Requirements met:

**Games and
Rules**

*Environment/
Materials:*

Activities:

Requirements met:

Webbing from Topical to Developmental Themes

Use a web format to compare how a topical theme in your curriculum uncovered the developmental themes of children. Sample webs are included below.

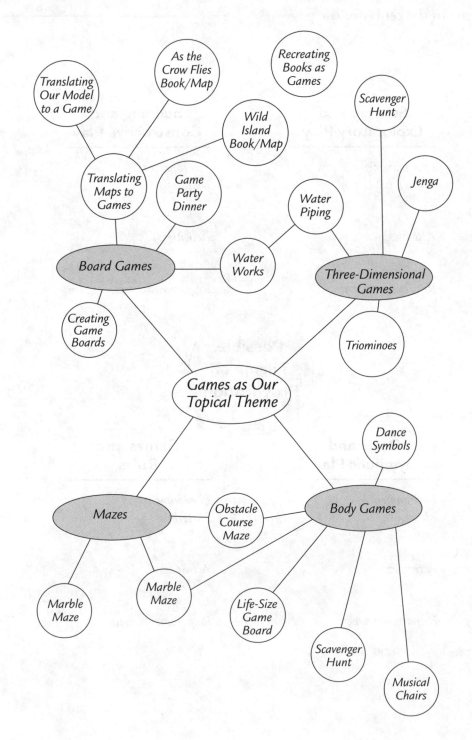

Evaluating Your Curriculum

As a professional, you need a method of regularly assessing the effectiveness of what you are doing. While you may be required to complete paperwork, it is important that you are also ensuring that your curriculum planning leads to what you value. Does it result in the expanded outcomes you are seeking for children? In different chapters throughout this handbook, we have been detailing a child-centered approach reflecting a variety of desired outcomes. Use the following consolidated form to assist you in assessing the results of your work.

Desired Outcomes for a Child-Centered Curriculum

Outcomes for Self-Concept and Social-Emotional Development

Identify specific indicators of children doing the following:

- ☐ forming strong bonds with significant adults
- ☐ feeling safe and secure
- ☐ seeing themselves as competent
- ☐ understanding and expressing their feelings and ideas
- ☐ understanding and participating in routines
- ☐ initiating their own activities
- ☐ taking on challenges
- ☐ forming relationships with their peers
- ☐ feeling a part of a group and helping others

Outcomes for Approaches to Learning

Identify specific indicators of children doing the following:

- ☐ showing motivation to learn something
- ☐ communicating clearly what they want through gestures and language
- ☐ demonstrating persistence
- ☐ using flexible problem-solving skills
- ☐ tolerating some frustration or delayed gratification

Outcomes for Learning about Learning

Identify specific indicators of children doing the following:

- ☐ wondering and showing curiosity
- ☐ using their bodies—mouths, fingers, hands, arms, legs—for exploring
- ☐ learning from their senses
- ☐ observing closely and noticing details
- ☐ comparing and sorting by looking carefully
- ☐ trying over and over again
- ☐ experimenting through trial and error, testing ideas
- ☐ using gestures and emerging language skill to share interests, questions, and ideas
- ☐ showing recognition and using past experiences for relationships and new learning

Outcomes for Complex Play Skills

Identify specific indicators of children doing the following:

- ☐ engaging peers and/or adults in play
- ☐ using props for their own play
- ☐ transforming space and materials to meet their needs
- ☐ negotiating with their peers
- ☐ adding language to their communications
- ☐ demonstrating an ability to focus and hold attention
- ☐ continuing focused play from day to day

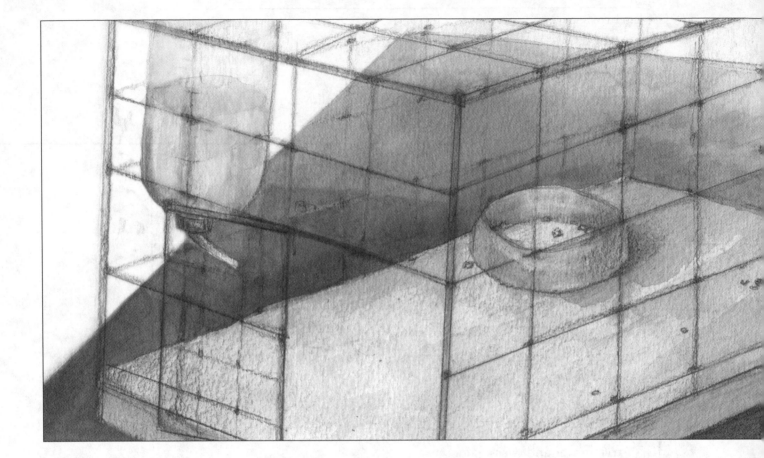

An Inspirational Story

The following story from preschool teacher Sarah A. Felstiner was written in 1996 for the first edition of this book. She writes about beginning her journey with using a child-centered emergent curriculum approach, documenting carefully with a tape recorder, camera, paper, and pens what unfolded. Read her self-reflections about the emerging guidelines she was developing for her teaching. Sarah's postscript, written over a decade later, reveals her to be even more reflective, with documentation becoming a cornerstone of her practice.

276

Look for Rikki Tikki at All Times:
The True Story of the Runaway Bunny

Sarah A. Felstiner, Preschool Teacher

> To be with children is to work one-third with certainty
> and two-thirds with uncertainty and the new.
> —Loris Malaguzzi, founder of the Reggio Emilia schools

When I begin a year of teaching, I have a choice of how to get from September to June. I can "drive," collecting maps and plotting my route by using lesson plans and a preformed curriculum. For me and my class, the journey will be predictable—I know what ground we'll cover and what we'll encounter along the way. We will be confined to a chosen path, making it impossible to follow any interesting turnoffs that we encounter along the way—essentially preventing any unplanned diversions that children, teachers, or parents might discover.

Instead, I try to "fly," to rise higher for a different perspective and allow the curriculum greater freedom of movement and direction. In flying, we may miss some of the details on the ground, but on the other hand, we'll get to appreciate the contours of the land, the tops of the mountains, the patchwork patterns of the fields.

Educationally, I'm talking about the difference between a preplanned, teacher-directed curriculum and one that is dynamic, experimental, and responsive to children's interests and needs.

My conviction of the need for an emergent curriculum was strengthened by my one-week visit to the remarkable preschools in Reggio Emilia, Italy. I had learned a great deal about these schools through articles, photos, slides, videos, and lectures by Reggio experts. These encounters pretty much convinced me that "the Reggio approach" was an ideal way to teach young children. But when I visited Reggio Emilia, educators there helped me see that it is not enough to simply find and implement an approach that impresses you and suits your personal style. Instead, you must do as they do in Reggio—make a commitment to continually question your techniques and philosophies through self-reflection, collaboration with your coworkers, and continual observation of the children you teach.

I knew that I couldn't and shouldn't try to replicate everything that was being done in the Reggio schools. Yet I wanted to look for the pieces of their approach that would be meaningful to my teaching and find ways to adapt those ideas for my use.

In that spirit, I returned to my classroom in California, determined to let children bring their ideas to the curriculum. I wanted each project, maybe even the whole year, to feel like one of those "teachable moments" when a child's genuine excitement becomes the basis for learning. This was my first step into emergent curriculum, filled with uncertainty and doubt, but eventually quite fulfilling. By the end of that school year, my experience with one runaway bunny had me completely convinced that the most genuine, effective, important curriculum in a preschool classroom is that which emerges from the needs and interests of the children.

Our pet rabbit, Rikki Tikki, was a much-loved friend, and children in the class visited him daily in his large outdoor hutch. One Monday morning, however, we returned to school to find that the door of Rikki Tikki's cage had been pried open and our cherished friend was gone. Matt, the first child to wander over to say good morning to the rabbit, discovered the empty cage and immediately reported it to me. I was shocked and upset. How should I respond to this news? How could I handle this situation? What do I say when Matt asks, "What happened?"

Perhaps because of the strangeness of the situation or perhaps due to the influence of my new Italian friends or perhaps because I am, above all, honest with the children in my class, I responded, "I don't know." Then I listened to the children's ideas, using a tape recorder, camera, and paper and pens to document their words and images about what happened to Rikki Tikki.

The ideas came pouring out. Children speculated that coyotes had come to open the cage, or that Rikki Tikki had pushed his way out. Some thought he had gone to find some rabbit friends; some thought he was searching for his mother. Many children were convinced that he must still be somewhere in our yard. Because a few other outdoor items were strewn about the play yard, I thought perhaps the cage had been pried open by human visitors, but I chose not to impose my hypothesis.

The children's ideas and suggestions were followed by actions. Some dug holes in the sand area and placed a piece of carrot at the bottom of each hole to lure Rikki Tikki back. Others built traps out of loose tires and climbing boards. Some began searching for clues with magnifying glasses and binoculars. Some were organizers. Jacqueline climbed to the top of the slide to call a meeting. Davis stood next to the empty cage and yelled, "Look for Rikki Tikki at all times!" Some children started drawing signs, maps, clues, and pictures of the missing rabbit—anything to help us find Rikki Tikki. But at the end of the first day, Rikki Tikki was still missing.

Over the next few weeks, many children used the paper and pens I brought outside each day. They drew elaborate maps that showed landmarks in our yard, footprints, and escape routes. They drew many pictures of Rikki Tikki, which they showed to parents, friends, and office staff, enlisting their help in the search. Writing skills blossomed as older children made signs that read "Lost rabbit" and "Thank you all for looking for Rikki Tikki," to post on the trees in our play yard. Some children wrote and drew letters for the rabbit and put them in a mailbox created just for Rikki Tikki. Even the youngest children began to add two long pointy ears to their basic scribbles and shapes. One small group collaborated on a flyer announcing the loss of our rabbit and describing his appearance. They made and colored multiple copies, posting them in and around the school.

Throughout this busy time, very few children even considered that we might not retrieve our rabbit. Books such as *The Runaway Bunny* and *Peter Rabbit* were read often and came to have special meaning, perhaps because their rabbit protagonists return home in the end. For most children, it was just a question of looking hard enough, trying the right things, not giving up. Long after the adults inwardly considered the rabbit gone for good, the children still searched for tracks, explored the yard, and took search parties to other classrooms. I supported and extended their ideas, providing the materials and supervision necessary for them to carry out their plans. Only after several weeks had passed did I begin to hear suggestions like "Maybe we should just get another bunny."

Then one morning in May, about a month after Rikki Tikki disappeared, I heard a rumor from another teacher that a parent in the school had seen our flyers and had also seen a sign posted at another school across the street announcing a found rabbit. Doubting that Rikki Tikki might still be around a month later, and not wanting to raise hopes too high, one teacher and two children went across the street to investigate. They came back saying the rabbit looked awfully familiar. Another group went over with some drawings they had done and a photo of the rabbit to confirm his identity. In talking to the staff at the school across the street, I learned that they had been keeping him there for three weeks and were just days away from taking him to the Humane Society. Word gradually spread among the children that Rikki Tikki had been found, and they got busy decorating his hutch with ribbons, paintings, and posters in preparation for his return. And of course they insisted that the broken door of his hutch be fixed.

The next morning, a small group of children along with the teacher set out with a carrying cage loaded on a red wagon. They crossed the street to the other school, lifted Rikki Tikki in, and wheeled him back. Before they even reached the door of the classroom, a crowd began to gather, and by the time they were all the way inside, the whole class was clustered around the small cage, calling to Rikki Tikki and touching his brown fur.

This incredible story of a real runaway bunny is what prompted me to analyze the ways I allow curriculum to develop in my classroom. I had to ask myself, "What if the pet rabbit doesn't escape next year? What if I don't even have a rabbit? How am I supposed to recreate that level of energy and engagement?" The experience with Rikki Tikki showed me that something special was happening in the classroom, and in thinking over the whole year, I realized that what I'd developed was a constant willingness to collaborate with the children. Through my efforts at letting the curriculum emerge from the children's interests, I had arrived at some basic guidelines for my teaching.

Honesty: I could have stifled the children's natural reactions and stunted their learning process by making up answers to their questions about Rikki Tikki's disappearance. I could have replaced him with a new rabbit right away or claimed that he'd gone to "rabbit heaven." I could have diverted children's interest with unrelated songs and activities about bunnies or distracted them with a different curriculum theme altogether. Instead, I responded with honesty and genuine feeling, allowing their questions to guide our search.

Trust: I let the children be my guide. I followed at their pace, in the direction they wanted to go. I discovered it is adults, not children, who have the short attention span. The children were willing to keep looking and keep working. Their involvement grew deeper with each day that went by. I had lost faith, but the children never stopped believing they would find Rikki Tikki.

Responsiveness: Throughout the year, children learned that I was a valuable resource—that they could take the initiative, and I would respond with eagerness. I was not so much a teacher as I was a colearner and fellow researcher. For me, that meant treating each new suggestion with some degree of seriousness and trying to decide which ones were possible to pursue.

Risk: The Rikki Tikki project was a perfect demonstration of the axiom that the greatest risk brings the greatest reward. When I began to acknowledge that the children were guiding the curriculum, I felt both anxious and excited. For me, flying feels less safe than driving, perhaps because in flight I have to leave the reliable stability of the ground and relinquish control of the pace and direction of travel. As a teacher, I feel this same risk when I abandon preset plans and expectations and allow children to help steer the curriculum in new directions. In this case, there was certainly no guarantee that our hunt for Rikki Tikki would come to a happy end, but as a teacher, I felt gratified when it did. On some cosmic level, I felt rewarded for pursuing this unplanned project and allowing it to fly. But actually, it doesn't matter whether the rabbit came back or not. The best thing I did for that group of children was to value their process and to pay attention to what happened along the way.

Observation: I was a careful watcher and listener throughout the project. In addition to investigating the mystery at hand, I sought opportunities for each child to grow within the experience. New skills were developed, new leaders emerged, and social groups changed and expanded.

Documentation: I took many, many photographs, saved a lot of artwork, and continually wrote down children's words, because that documentation served as an ever-growing record of our search. In addition, my attentive observation and record keeping demonstrated to the children that I valued the work they were doing. At the same time, this documentation—compiled on a constantly changing bulletin board within the classroom—served to reassure parents that their children were busily working, playing, and learning. Many parents became involved in the search and the saga, often bringing pictures and maps to school that children had made at home.

They reported on new theories that had come up in family conversation. This was my evidence that the curriculum was expanding beyond the walls of the classroom and that the children and I were developing into a learning community.

Collaboration: Collaboration among and between children, teachers, and parents was at the heart of all of this work. Collaboration requires honesty, trust, and responsiveness. Collaboration creates risk when we willingly share the reins with all the coteachers, children, and family members in our class—imagine fifty riders working to steer the same horse! But through observation, documentation, and collaboration with the children, I had one of the most successful teaching and learning experiences of my life.

I believe strongly that children deserve to be the authors of their own curriculum, but I still wish for more order and predictability than a truly emergent approach seems to provide. My struggle as a teacher is to find ways to make the work in my classroom feel both organized and spontaneous, both grounded and free. The compromise I've chosen is to promote emergent projects while carefully documenting children's work. By recording children's words, images, and activities, I not only facilitate their own learning, but I demonstrate to myself and to other adults the value of their emergent curriculum.

2010 Postscript: Looking Back, Looking Forward

Looking back at this story from over a decade ago, it's reassuring to find that I've become more comfortable with the uncertainty inherent in an emergent approach to curriculum design. There's nothing like a repeated cycle of anxiety followed by success to build one's confidence. Time after time over these past years, I've leapt into the unknown, and each time I've landed somewhere new, revealing, precious. Now I really don't care what the children and I end up investigating; what matters to me is the quality of the investigation. I've stopped measuring my years by "How much did we cover?" and started evaluating how richly and deeply we explored whatever topics the children brought my way.

The idea that seems underemphasized in what I wrote a decade ago is the immeasurable value of collaboration among teachers in facilitating an emergent curriculum. I'm embarrassed that the names of my coteachers didn't appear in that essay. Roberta Immordino, Diane Guthrie, Kirsten Wright, and Kitti Pecka were my friends and mentors throughout this miraculous story of Rikki Tikki's disappearance and return. A newer discovery for me is the critical value of collecting traces of children's work during the course of the project. These documents are the cornerstone for the discussions and interactive planning sessions that teachers need to facilitate emergent work. At my current school, teachers meet each week to pore over photos, drawings, scribbled notes, and audio or video recordings. We work together to tease out the questions children are trying to answer and the underlying themes that drive their play. Next steps and new provocations are generated directly from teachers' shared analysis of these primary sources.

The other benefit that more years of practicing this approach has brought me is a rich archive of written stories documenting each in-depth investigation. These books, of course, are a gift to the children who lived the project and a way to communicate that work to their families. But they serve another purpose as well—proof that intense thinking and high-caliber learning are happening as a direct result of this organic, dynamic approach. When prospective parents tour the school, I show them these stories and explain, "We won't be using spelling workbooks or offering direct math instruction, but just look at all the rich literacy and numeracy that grew out of these investigations." And when our licensor asks to see our lesson plans for the year, I reply, "I can't tell you exactly what we'll be doing three weeks from Friday, but I can promise you that it will be exactly as rich as the stories you see here."

Share Your Reflections with Sarah

Write a letter to Sarah at SarahatHilltop@gmail.com with your reflections on how she was learning to negotiate the curriculum to respect the children's themes as well as uphold her own values and dispositions. Consider including your thoughts about the following:

- How did Sarah's disposition for predictability and planned experiences challenge her as she worked toward an emergent curriculum approach? What changes in her disposition has she made in the last decade?

- What did Sarah discover about the power of collaboration with the children and her coworkers?

- What role does documentation play in Sarah's curriculum approach?

- What specific examples did you read about the "deep learning" that the children experienced with Sarah's approach?

▸ *Practice What You've Learned*

Practice Becoming Articulate about Your Curriculum Approach

At some point, you will probably have to explain or defend your curriculum to others in conversations or presentations. You can use details from your documentation and evidence from the evaluation of your curriculum as resources for communicating the value of a child-centered approach. Use the following activities to develop yourself as a spokesperson and advocate for meaningful emergent curriculum.

Practice responding to these statements and questions to sharpen your skills for describing how your curriculum is meeting children's interests, parent concerns, and early learning guidelines.

1. I can't tell if my child is learning anything in your class if she doesn't bring home art projects or work sheets every day.

2. I brought you these flash cards that are supposed to be good for developing babies' brains.

3. If you don't plan an activity for each part of the day, won't the kids just get bored with free play?

4. What if my child just wants to play with blocks all day and not learn anything?

5. Are you going to teach my child to read in this class?

6. My child is a typical "terrible two"; feel free to put him on time-out whenever he deserves it.

When families enroll their children in your program, you can give them some initial written information about your approach to curriculum planning, inviting them to join you in ongoing dialogue. You can also set up an e-mail distribution list or blog for ongoing written communication with families. Because writing a curriculum statement in a concise manner is not always easy, use the following activity to develop your writing skills for this task. Work alone or in a small group to develop an initial letter to families regarding your approach to curriculum planning. This initial work will serve as a reference point for your ongoing written communications, whatever form they take.

1. Brainstorm a list of points to include.

2. Decide on priorities, grouping related points together.

3. Number the order in which you wish to cover the points.

4. Write a paragraph for each set of points.

5. Write your final copy.

Notes about Your Planning and Communication

Use the space below to make notes about how you communicate your planning approach. Use the questions to help you get started.

What are you most confident about in communicating your approach to curriculum planning?

_____

_____

_____

_____

_____

_____

_____

What skills do you want to strengthen in yourself?

_____

_____

_____

_____

_____

_____

_____

Developing Yourself 9

 A child-centered emergent approach to curriculum is a lifestyle—a set of beliefs and values that influence teaching behaviors.

Beginning Reflections

Think of a time when you had to make a significant change in your life and you were successful. Remember the details of what that success was like—remember the feelings, sounds, and people involved.

What kept you motivated to stay on track?

_____

_____

_____

Were there mentors or role models whom you looked to?

_____

_____

_____

How did you get through times of stress and discouragement?

_____

_____

_____

What kept you learning and growing?

_____

_____

_____

A Journey of Personal and Professional Development

A child-centered emergent approach to curriculum isn't just a method or teaching technique. It is a lifestyle—a set of beliefs and values that influence teaching behaviors. This approach requires a complex set of skills and knowledge and, most importantly, particular attitudes and dispositions.

You probably spent your school years as a student in teacher-directed, rule-focused classrooms. Your own experience of education is most likely contrary to what you want to be doing with children. Using a child-centered approach requires that you recreate a new vision of education.

Whether you work in a home- or center-based program, you must reinvent the role of the teacher. You must begin to trust yourself and the children you work with to keep growing and learning. You must be willing to go up against the status quo, to challenge and advocate for meaningful learning environments for yourself and the children.

New Roles for Providers and Teachers

Most people enter the early childhood field with ideas about the role they can play in children's learning. They want to pass along knowledge, shape children's minds, do fun crafts, and get children ready for school and future jobs. With this in mind, they tend to use the only model they are familiar with—school. In an attempt to make "educational" activities more developmentally appropriate, well-meaning teachers water down activities traditionally done with children in the primary grades.

At this point in our country's history, childhood is under assault and has been seriously eroded. Our schools have failed many children. Efforts to reform schools are often making the problems even more challenging with proscribed school readiness curriculum and high-stakes testing. In an age of information technology, the kind of learning children need to engage in goes far beyond the traditional way our schools have educated children. Children in early childhood education settings deserve something much more profound than lessons on colors and holiday crafts. To engage with academic content, young children need more than information to recite and check boxes on an assessment form.

Today the real needs of children in early education include the following:

- real relationships with adults who trust and believe in them

- real time to pursue their curiosities, questions, and skills

- real work, not meaningless chores or projects

- real intellectual engagement, not rote academic tasks

- real understandings of how content knowledge will be of interest and use

- real things to develop their bodies, not subdue them

- real guidance and coaching, not shaming, punishment, and isolation

- real role models, not superheroes or celebrities
- real reflections of their lives, not commercial or cartoon renditions

Teachers who are truly providing a child-centered curriculum are playing different roles than the typical ones of cheerleader, taskmaster, disciplinarian, and timekeeper. Planning curriculum along the lines described in this handbook requires a different way of thinking about adult roles and behaviors.

You can begin by thinking about yourself in some new ways. Elizabeth Jones and Gretchen Reynolds, college instructors and authors who have written extensively about the value of play in early childhood education, have provoked us to think of the roles of the teacher in some new ways. How is what you do like the work of an archaeologist, broadcaster, advocate, improvisational artist, or scientist? The better you get at articulating what you do, the more effective you become in securing the respect and compensation that comes with these jobs. Consider the "Teacher as . . ." examples on the following pages.

Teacher as Architect

Consider how an architect thinks and approaches his job in designing buildings. You can bring a similar eye to the environments you design in your program.

- Evaluate a space based on a child's-eye view.
- Adapt a space to the children's play needs and interests.
- Create opportunities to explore light and shadow, sound, color, and texture.
- Integrate outdoor and natural world elements into the indoor environment.
- Rearrange the environment to create new interest in each area.
- Plan the outdoor space as carefully as the indoor space.

Teacher as Observer

Keen observation skills are essential for many jobs, including those of scientists, artists, engineers, and therapists. How might the observation skills of an ornithologist or gardener apply to your work as an early childhood educator?

- Become a field researcher in child development.
- Appreciate the details of children's complex play.
- Note a child's likes, dislikes, accomplishments, and frustrations.
- Observe before intervening or reacting.
- Plan curriculum experiences from children's interests and ideas.
- Spot ways to integrate academic content into everyday experiences.

Teacher as Prop Manager

Behind the scenes of every production (be it theater, film, sports event, or gourmet meal), you'll find people who specialize in managing all the props, costumes, supplies, and needed equipment. These folks make other people's work go smoothly. Teachers can take on the role of prop manager to help children be successful in mastering the play skills that will keep them motivated and successful in their endeavors.

- Arrange materials to suggest and encourage play possibilities.
- Supply props as "invitations" in anticipation of play scripts.
- Select materials that lend themselves to open-ended use and transformation.
- Casually pick up and put away props to help create order behind the play.
- Provide additional materials without interrupting the play flow.

Teacher as Mediator

When people work, play, or live together, at some point their interests or different perspectives are likely to clash and they need a third party to help work things out. When early childhood teachers assume the role of mediator, they offer support and model how to negotiate different ideas or needs.

- Create a climate of safety for children to express their feelings and ideas.
- Use conflicts as opportunities to learn social skills.
- Provide support and language for children to solve their own problems.

- Focus on the content of the play rather than on violation of rules.

- Interpret and facilitate children's communication with each other.

Teacher as Coach

While some teacher roles, such as architect or prop manager, are behind the scenes, children also benefit from an out-front coach who is attentive to individual needs as well as the scope and sequence of acquiring particular skills. Effective coaches not only cheer people on but also convey a belief and trust in who they work with.

- Recognize children's strengths and provide opportunities to practice them.

- Encourage risk taking with a supportive presence.

- Introduce skills to support self-selected tasks.

- Match challenges to individual interests.

- Promote teamwork with materials and activities that require group effort.

Teacher as Scribe

Because many young children haven't developed writing skills, the teacher becomes the scribe who records things that are being said and done.

- Model that the spoken word can be written down and read.

- Take photos and make written and pictorial representations of children's play and language.

- Document and archive stories about children's play activities to have as a reference or memory book in the future.

- Take dictation or transcribe children's language.

- Support children's efforts to tell stories or write about their play or creations.

- Involve children in using technology to document and revisit experiences.

Teacher as Scientist

A scientist has a curious mind and is always wondering "why" and "what if." When teachers employ a scientific mind-set, they discover new possibilities for themselves and the children.

- Wonder and ask questions.
- Study observable evidence.
- Consider other perspectives and evidence not seen.
- Collect data and look for patterns.
- Hypothesize, try out hunches, and examine the results.
- Communicate findings.

Teacher as Broadcaster

While one role for a teacher is that of scribe or journalist, another is to extend with broadcasting what you are seeing and hearing. And because we know how discouraging it is to hear only bad news broadcasts, let's focus our teacher broadcasting on the good news that is unfolding—things children are showing or teaching us, their investigations, accomplishments, creativity, skill, and exuberant engagement in relationships.

- Spread the news of the play stories you observe in your group.

- Collect and display examples of children's activities and creations.

- Represent a child's point of view about a significant event.

- Share children's good ideas with others.

- Communicate with families about the learning embedded in their child's chosen play.

- Set up blogs and other web-based communication systems.

Self-Assessment

What behaviors are part of your daily caregiving and teaching? Use this checklist to assess yourself.

- ☐ I focus on building a strong relationship with each child and family in my group.
- ☐ I monitor the influence of my own values, background, and hot buttons when I am planning and in my responses to children, families, and coworkers.
- ☐ I ask myself questions about the meaning of children's play and provide additional props to keep play going.
- ☐ I mediate conflict to promote continuous self-initiated play.
- ☐ I allow messes when related to productive play.
- ☐ I maintain order behind the scenes to keep the play going.
- ☐ I avoid interventions that sidetrack children's play activities.
- ☐ I tell stories using children's play themes during group times.
- ☐ I incorporate children's passions into curriculum planning and community building.
- ☐ I enthusiastically document and discuss children's play with coworkers and families.
- ☐ I am playful in interactions and share my own interests with children.
- ☐ I regularly collaborate with my coworkers and look for different perspectives.
- ☐ I continually study how children can acquire knowledge within the different academic domains through their play.
- ☐ I am developing my voice as an educator and advocate, orally and in writing.
- ☐ I pursue ways to continually grow as a professional.

Review your responses, then set goals for gaining new knowledge and skills you want to acquire. For example:

- Seek out websites, workshops, classes, and professional conferences.
- Visit other programs.
- Participate in study tours.
- Find a mentor—someone who can serve as a model, coach, and peer consultant for you. (If you have checked most of the items above, consider becoming a mentor for someone else.)

Cultivating Your Dispositions

Intentional teachers in child-centered programs have certain qualities that distinguish them from teachers who depend on curriculum activity books, follow the same theme plans year after year, or struggle daily to get the children involved in anything productive. The knowledge and skills of master teachers are not necessarily different from those of other teachers. Rather, these professionals have become improvisational artists. They have developed a set of attitudes and habits of mind that enable them to respond readily to the classroom dynamics and multiple needs of children.

Lilian Katz refers to these habits of mind or tendencies to respond to certain situations in certain ways as dispositions. *Merriam-Webster's Collegiate Dictionary* defines disposition as a "prevailing tendency, mood, or inclination; a temperamental makeup; and the tendency . . . to act in a certain manner under given circumstances." Curiosity, friendliness, bossiness, passivity, cynicism, and creativity are dispositions rather than skills or a kind of knowledge.

Explore this idea of dispositions by completing the "Dispositions for Child-Centered Teachers" form on the following page. First, think about yourself or a specific teacher with whom you work. Get a clear picture in your mind of that teacher's or your own typical facial and verbal expressions and body language. Where do you usually find yourself or this teacher in the classroom? Then mark where you think you or that teacher falls on each continuum.

Dispositions for Child-Centered Teachers

Directions: Mark where you or the teacher you have chosen falls on each disposition continuum. Review your answers and then answer the question at the end.

Has a mind-set about children that reveals curiosity and delight in who they are and what they do.	Seems to like kids but can't tell you why.	Approaches children primarily to correct or direct them in an activity.
Values play, plans for it in setting up the environment, and watches closely to see what the children do.	Lets play happen in the classroom, so as to have time to tend to other teacher chores.	Views free play as time for children to "blow off steam" in between teacher-directed activities.
Expects children to change and challenge plans and remains flexible to follow their interests and questions.	Allows children to briefly digress from planned activities but then gets them back on task.	Is highly invested in having teacher-planned activities carried out by the children.
Is willing to try new things and take risks for the benefit of the children's and her own learning as a teacher.	Seldom initiates anything with children outside of tried and true activities.	Has his own way of doing things and resists new ways and ideas.
Continually examines experiences and her own actions in search of new understandings.	Rolls with the punches and doesn't think much more about it.	Doesn't see his own role or impact on classroom events; tends to see others as the cause of things not going well.
Is alert and active in addressing a bias or the limitations of the status quo.	May agree when a bias is pointed out or a change is called for, but is reluctant to speak or upset anyone.	Doesn't notice and thus participates in perpetuating bias and the limitations of the status quo.
Actively seeks collaboration and believes two heads are better than one.	Is pleased when asked to join in, but it doesn't occur to her to seek out collaboration.	Has his own way of doing things and prefers to work alone.

What changes would you like to see?

Useful Dispositions to Acquire

Throughout this handbook, you have read about different aspects of child-centered curricula that are thoughtfully implemented after careful observation and planning. You have read about ways teachers and family child care providers can support children's learning by providing meaningful experiences. A number of useful dispositions can help you as you move into a more child-centered emergent curriculum. Cultivate these dispositions in yourself, and you will find that creating child-centered programs and curricula will come more naturally.

Be Curious about Children's Learning and Development

Most early childhood educators enjoy children and their learning process. This enjoyment is a primary motivation for taking on the responsibility of working with young children. Once on the job, however, teachers too commonly lose that sense of delight. It is quickly diminished by the pressures of trying to conduct activities, manage behaviors, and complete required paperwork. Adults soon become more focused on the goals of their curriculum plans or their requirements than on the children's learning process. Typically, teachers jump to control misbehavior rather than ponder the reasons for a child's actions. Delight and curiosity come easily when you truly watch children. Curiosity leads to more job satisfaction and professional growth.

Value Children's Play

Play is of value in and of itself, but adults easily lose track of this fact. Children who are independently involved in play often go unnoticed by teachers, who use this time for other pressing needs in their job (such as record keeping, housekeeping, resource gathering, or consulting with a coworker, parent, or supervisor).

Teachers who value play recognize that the best curriculum emerges out of the themes children are investigating and expressing, rather than from a commercial activity book or a file of last year's curriculum plans. When teachers can identify the kinds of play occurring in their classrooms, they deepen their understandings of child development and get better at planning for individual children and overall intellectual engagement.

Expect Continuous Change and Challenge

The nature of early childhood involves intense change and challenge. This is the context for the daily work of educators, requiring them to make continuous on-the-spot decisions and judgment calls. Teachers respond more effectively when they expect constant changes and challenges and make them central to their work. They learn to recognize their own hot buttons and then to just "go with the flow."

Be Willing to Take Risks and Make Mistakes

As you come to expect continuous change and challenge, a willingness to take risks and make mistakes naturally follows. Without this disposition you won't grow. Children benefit from seeing this behavior modeled so they, too, will be willing to take a safe risk and not have their self-esteem or self-confidence undermined by making mistakes.

Make Time for Regular Reflection and Self-Examination

People learn from reflecting on experience and from analyzing events, dynamics, and conclusions. You also learn from comparing the "official word" or theory with your own intuition and experience. Reflection may confirm or contradict previous understandings. Either way, it deepens insights and the disposition toward seeing yourself as a lifelong learner.

Teachers who are not predisposed to self-reflection and evaluation tend to attribute all classroom difficulties to someone else—it's the children who are too immature, disrespectful, or out of control. Even if that's true, it is only half of the story. You need to gain perspective on how your behaviors, expectations, and patterns from your own childhood impact the situations you set up for children. So create a time and place each day for some intentional reflection and self-examination.

Seek Collaboration, Mentoring, and Peer Support

Though working with children can be delightful, it can also be isolating. Regular discussion with peers and mentors helps you sustain your self-reflection process and learn the value of different approaches. These conversations can involve getting feedback on ideas, sharing teaching

strategies, and gaining support. Joining with colleagues, you can make changes in yourself and in your working conditions, compensation, and the quality of care and education for children.

Be a Professional Watchdog and a Whistle-Blower

Family child care providers and classroom teachers are under tremendous pressure to meet other people's needs. It is not only children who present you with numerous demands; it is also parents, coworkers, and supervisors. On top of that, add the pressure from standards and assessments for school readiness. Without a solid footing in the learning theories, cultural awareness, and child development, you can easily slip into accepting a "pushdown," biased academic curriculum.

Embolden yourself to become an advocate for children and for your own needs as a teacher. You will feel proud when you speak up to question decisions, policies, and regulations that are headed down the wrong path.

Practice Identifying Dispositions

Read through the following scenario and look for the dispositions these people display.

The Bucket

A family child care provider, Naomi, and her assistant, Sandria, are supervising children in the backyard. Three four-year-old children are playing together on the climber. They are using a rope to lift a metal bucket full of sand to the top of the climber platform.

Sandria tells Naomi, "I've told those kids to stop using the bucket that way. I think it's too dangerous."

"I feel a bit nervous about how safe that is too," Naomi responds, "but let's watch what they do for a moment before we stop them."

"Look how they figured out how to tie the rope to the bucket and then around the climber," says Sandria. "They've invented a complex system, almost like a pulley."

"And look how much cooperation it's taking to get the bucket to the top without spilling the sand. This activity seems too valuable to stop," Naomi observes. "What can we do to make it safer?"

Sandria replies, "Maybe we can exchange the metal bucket for a plastic one so it won't be so dangerous if it falls or hits someone."

A Closer Look

Rather than quickly reacting to and stopping the children's play, these providers have taken time to observe, reflect, and analyze the value of what is happening. Sandria and Naomi are conscientious about safety concerns, but they weigh the risks in light of the value of these children's investigation and cooperative play. They collaborate and find a solution, allowing for an acceptable risk in order for the children's learning to continue.

A Commitment to Ongoing Self-Evaluation and Growth

Before you can really implement a child-centered approach, you must examine your own attitudes and experiences and take steps to rid your curriculum of meaningless activities and tired ideas. Children need teachers who are passionate, curious, joyful, and committed to being fully mindful. Following are some ideas to cultivate these qualities in yourself.

Learning from Children

Careful observations remind us that children approach the world with a fresh and open attitude. Children explore with wonder and excitement because they are experiencing things for the first time. They haven't yet become accustomed to the adult confines of discouragement, deadened senses, lowered self-esteem, or lack of confidence.

Reclaim your own wonder by learning from children involved in activities like those that follow.

Sam, ten months old, intently grabs at his shadow, made by the sun streaming through the window above him. Then he puts his face down and touches the shadow with his tongue and lips.

Amber, a toddler, puts her whole body into the sensory table filled with macaroni. She moves back and forth through the macaroni, laughing with delight as she hears the sound it makes.

Diego, two years old, runs up a small grassy hill and rolls down. He gets up and does this again and again, laughing joyously as he rolls.

Jasmine, three years old, is at the easel carefully brushing paint over the entire surface of her forearm. She then moves the brush to her hand, painting each finger, covering the front, back, and nails.

Casey, eight years old, and Randy, thirteen years old, use the hose to create a giant mud puddle in the field behind the house. Both jump in joyfully, covering their entire bodies with the velvety stuff. They swish around awhile, then jump out and spray each other with icy water from the hose, squealing the entire time. Once clean, they jump right back in the mud and start over.

Cultivating Aesthetics

Children explore the world with all of their senses for learning and understanding as well as for the absolute delight of a sensory experience. As a teacher, you must reawaken your senses to gain more understanding of children and increase your own pleasures and quality of life. An effective starting place is naming what pleases you at a sensory level and describing what you like about it.

In *Art and Creative Development for Young Children* (2008), Robert Schirrmacher and Jill Englebright Fox define aesthetics as an abstract concept that means "perception" in Greek. Aesthetics, the authors state, offer a focused and metaphorical way of knowing and experiencing the world that involves an attitude, process, and response to objects and experiences.

Appreciating aesthetics is a basic human response that involves active engagement using all of the senses to relish an object or experience. This allows us to become completely lost and totally consumed in the moment. Aesthetics include an awareness and appreciation of the natural beauty found in nature, art, movement, music, and life.

Cultivating your aesthetic sense will not only heighten your appreciation of how children approach the world, but also will enrich your own life. Tending to aesthetics may require shifting how you move through the world and what you pay attention to and focus on. Once the process begins, your life will be flooded with new awareness:

- You'll revel in the quality of light at different times of the day and seasons.
- You'll want to touch the weaving of colors in the coat next to you.
- Your ear will hear a bird song that leaves you smiling.
- A perfectly ripe piece of melon will make its way from your fingers, across your lips and tongue, leaving its delicious juice for you to savor.

It is worth studying Schirrmacher and Engelbright Fox's discussion of the attitude, process, and responses to heighten your aesthetic sense. This study should involve not only your head but all of your senses.

The aesthetic *attitude* requires a willingness to stop and be involved in the present and to approach experiences with openness and childlike freshness. The aesthetic *process* involves intense focusing on the here and now, such as

- experiencing something as if for the very first time;
- listening attentively and getting lost in your senses;
- visually exploring and quietly contemplating;

- manipulating, feeling, and touching; and
- taking time to be with an experience.

Your *response* to aesthetic experiences builds your understandings and enhances your quality of life. Notice your emotions: You may feel a sense of wonder, appreciation, joy, surprise, awe, exhilaration. Notice your physiological response: Are you smiling, perspiring, shivering, slumping, alert? Notice your mental response: Have you formed any new ideas from this experience?

Practicing with Watercolors

To practice the aesthetic attitude, process, and response, work with a set of watercolor paints, using the following guidelines:

- Visually explore and notice the colors, individually and as they mix together.
- Examine the effect that different amounts of water have on the color. Notice how water spreads the color on the paper.
- Experiment with different ways to use the brush. How many ways can you spread the paint?
- Use different techniques to move the color across the paper—splotches, dots, drops, lines, shapes.
- Take your time and watch what occurs with each of your explorations, becoming as engaged in the process as you can.
- Notice your emotions as you work. How are you feeling?
- Notice your physiological response. What is your body doing and saying to you?
- Notice your mental response. Do you have any new ideas? How would you evaluate this experience?

An Inspirational Story

Ezra's challenges as a teacher began on his first day of work, but his ability to reflect and trust in his instinctive understandings kept him from giving up. Notice how he uses reflections on his detailed observations of children to fuel his courage and innovative practices. Consider the "secret ingredient" he identifies that keeps him growing as a professional, not just resigning himself to limits and regulations.

When Teachers Are Supported, the Amazing Will Happen

Ezra Stoker-Graham, Head Start Teacher

On my first day working with young children in a therapeutic child care center, I was spit on, cursed at, and kicked. Yet the next day I came back. Driven by my potential to make a strong, meaningful impact in children's lives, to be a positive male role model for many children who did not have a father at home, and to feel the joy that comes with simply playing with young children, I had found work I could believe in. Nevertheless, it took nearly ten years of working in different centers and taking classes before I found my professional home and a solid direction for my teaching.

I realize now that in the early years we stuffed too much into each day. If we were talking about snow, the children created a home for a snowman, snow books filled the library, shaving cream (snow) and cars were put in the sensory tub. What I saw but did not have the knowledge or courage to articulate was that the teachers I worked with were creating these environments because they were guessing the children would like them or because they had always made them. They were not making them because it was something the children had shown interest in. The culminating moment that helped me understand what I was feeling happened when the teachers came into the classroom on a Saturday to transform our indoor climber into a fire truck. I wondered to myself, "Why aren't we building the fire truck *with* the children?"

During the four years I spent working in a center at a community college, I started hearing bits and pieces about emergent curriculum. My child development coordinator shared an article with me about a classroom that used a minimalist approach to the materials children were exposed to each day. The children created their own environment in relationship with the teacher. I realized that's what was missing—an authentic relationship with the children, a classroom the children had ownership in.

When I became the lead teacher at the community college, I was excited to implement some of these new ideas, but it didn't happen. I wasn't brave enough or experienced enough to confidently and clearly share my vision with my coteachers. Management was slow to support changes to a classroom culture that was deeply entrenched and respected. I felt alone. The hectic, high-pressured atmosphere made me depressed and edgy. I left that job confused, defeated, and wounded. I didn't know what I would do next. I didn't know if I even wanted to be a teacher anymore. But I needed to find another job quickly, so two weeks later I was back working with young children.

While working I took an advanced early childhood education class with Tom Drummond that opened my eyes to new possibilities. He introduced me to the project approach, and his genius was that he did it by immersing the class in a project approach—without telling us. He invited us to take a walking field trip to explore the wetlands on campus and suggested that we bring our notebooks and pens to write down our thoughts and observations. When we gathered together after our walk to share what we observed, the room became alive with excitement. Simply by giving us the power to create our own learning and investigate what moved us, Professor Drummond created a group of students eager to continue to explore a project on wetlands. I understood this wasn't really an environmental studies class, but rather an experience of excitement about learning that we could give to children. If we gave them the opportunity to explore what they were interested in and gave them the ability to build the curriculum from their own ideas, their learning would be rich and meaningful.

I went to work and began to observe the children more closely. I asked questions. I listened. Slowly, a project centering on pets emerged. The children drew pictures of their pets, wrote stories and poetry, created a pet book, made pet food in the sandbox, and developed graphs and charts about their pets. We took field trips and had a rescue dog visit our classroom. I fervently documented everything that was happening and finally created a documentation board that hung in the main lobby of the center. Confidently, I brought the center director to the documentation board and described what a joy it had been to immerse so deeply in learning with the children. She replied, "This is great. Now don't you think it's time to do something else?" Before this experience, her comment would have defeated me, but now it was too late. I had found love for my work again, and I knew the direction I wanted to go. I just needed a place to teach where this type of exploration by children would be encouraged.

In September 1999 I found the job that helped me put roots into my profession. I found a home in Highline Head Start. Immediately I knew this place was different. The teachers, family support workers, and managers were warm, professional, and determined to create a beacon in the community. The vision was to become an innovative, model Head Start program. We were encouraged to try new things. We were asked to be brave. The director and the child development and family support coordinators backed up the vision with actions. We were offered training about the schools of Reggio Emilia, with inspiring early childhood authors as guest speakers. We had in-depth discussions about emergent curriculum. A trip to a Reggio-inspired program, Chicago Commons, proved to be an epiphany for me and my teaching. We were awestruck by the beauty of the classrooms and astonished by the thorough, focused projects the children had completed. The teachers' meticulous cycle of observing children, making hypotheses, trying an idea inspired by the children's play, and then observing again impressed us. We could see the children in the classroom. We knew who they were through immaculate documentation panels that revealed tremendous depth.

This is what many of us were craving. We wanted to transform our classrooms into beautiful places that respected and inspired children. We wanted to develop a highly intentional curriculum that was responsive to children. We wanted to explore the hearts and minds of children, but we wondered how to make this monumental change possible within our current Head Start structure. First, we wondered how to create such huge change in our environment and in our practice while meeting the Head Start requirements. How do we document relentlessly in family files, track health and nutrition information, conduct monthly staffings, support monthly family events, and fit emergent curriculum into the boxes of the required lesson plan? Second, we tried to figure out how to do this work within the structure of one teacher and one assistant teacher per classroom.

Talking with my coworker and friend Bev about how to create lasting change, we realized the only way to sustain this work would be to do it together. So we walked into our fearless, twinkling-eyed director's office and pitched the following idea: Instead of two teachers for eighteen children, we would have four teachers for thirty-six children. We would open the door between the two classrooms and allow the children to flow between the two rooms. We would create a beautiful space that would have an enormous block area, multiple easels, a huge art center, a well-stocked writing center, and soft places for children to relax and look at books or talk with friends. We would use four teachers to our advantage, following different children's interests in a small group with one teacher, while another teacher took a small group of children outside and the other teachers observed children's play. Despite the fact that we had thirty-six children, the classroom would feel alive and energetic without being overwhelming. And finally, the key to making this work was that the four teachers would meet after class four days a week for thirty minutes. In that time we would share what we saw the children doing, the successes, the struggles, the possible new avenues to follow, and then we would make assignments for each of us for the next day.

Our director did not cut us down with doubt or cynicism. He did not question how we could do this and still meet Head Start requirements. He simply listened and told us to make it happen. He emboldened us with his trust and his faith. He exuded the belief and confidence in us as teachers that we would imbue into the children in our classroom.

Elated and determined to develop our vision, we talked and planned and dreamed together. Because our management team supported us, we could throw out the old lesson plan and build one that opened space for us to become more intentional in our approach. We asked on the new lesson plan: What are the children excited about? What are they struggling with? What are the successes? How can volunteers support the classroom? What is emerging?

We agreed on a schedule that offered a consistent beginning and end to the day. The children would eat breakfast in the same room every day. Next, they would participate in a morning meeting where we would plan the day together. As the morning meetings finished in each room, the door between the two rooms would open and one classroom for thirty-six children would materialize. For an hour and a half, children would flow between the two rooms. They could paint, write stories, draw pictures, build with blocks, dance, sing, play instruments, meet in small groups to focus on a shared interest, read stories, count, pretend, climb and jump, investigate, explore, negotiate, and form strong and faithful friendships.

Just as in any classroom, some days were rough and uneven. There were shaky moments and times of confusion on just how to make our idea work, but we never felt pressure from the management team to revert to the old structure. We were trusted and encouraged. On most days in our open-door classroom, there was a hum—a whirring joyfulness of children deeply engaged in their play. There was rhythm and dance to each day. Every day was new. Every day the children knew they could build their learning in relationship with the teachers.

When I think back on that school year, I am filled with a sense of contentment and strength. The freedom we had to transform our environment, our practice, and ourselves will always be a treasured time in my career. The most indelible memory of that entire year, however, came at the very beginning. On September 11, 2001, six days before our experiment began, the world changed. The Twin Towers tumbled in New York City. Airplanes crashed into the Pentagon and in a field in Pennsylvania. We were frightened, distressed, and shaken, but we were also hopeful as children arrived for the first day.

The power and the blessing of our new approach to truly know the children during this unsettling time was profound. As we watched and listened to the children, we began to see the events of September 11 emerging throughout the classroom. In the block area over and over and over again, children built two towers of equal height and used their hand or another block to knock them down. At the easel, children painted skyscrapers burning a brilliant orange and red. With fine-tipped markers, they drew stunningly detailed pictures of people falling out of buildings. They wrote stories about watching the news with their families. They wrote stories about fighting bad men in the dark.

As this poignant play and expression emerged, we planned opportunities to write and draw and talk about what the children were feeling. During the small groups, it was difficult not to weep at times as the children told their stories with blazing truth. We collected their work and created a documentation panel of our story. First, it lived in our classroom. Then it traveled to the main hall of our office where more people saw it. Finally, our documentation panel told its story at a local library for a few months.

I will always be grateful that our open-door classroom began in the fall of 2001, because I had three teachers to plan with, mourn with, and heal with. Although I still had much to learn, and still do, I am glad that I was part of a teaching team that endeavored to be in authentic relationships with children. I'm glad that we faced the pain of the time with honesty. I'm thankful that the children had a safe outlet to express what they needed to express.

We were able to do so in the context of Head Start because we had fearless management who encouraged innovation, valued teachers, and respected children. We were given the freedom to try, and we were given meaningful support. But what about meeting all of the Head Start requirements while growing this new idea? This is the secret: When teachers are treated with respect, when they are believed in, when they are given the freedom to grow, to do big work that inspires them, and when their work is joyful, then meeting the requirements does not feel burdensome. When teachers are trusted and supported with concrete actions, such as allowing a lesson plan to be changed, they feel buoyed to respond with exemplary work. When teachers and management work together with a united passion and purpose—listening to children, loving children, and celebrating childhood—the amazing will happen.

Share Your Reflections with Ezra

Write a letter to Ezra at EStokerGrahamReflect@gmail.com with your reflections on how he was learning to negotiate the curriculum to respect the children's themes as well as overcome the barriers to an emergent approach. Consider including your thoughts about the following:

- What aspects of Ezra's journey helped him cultivate his passion for his work and overcome the challenges to child-centered practices?
- How did collaboration with his coworkers support Ezra in his work?

- What insights has Ezra discovered about the importance of teachers having freedom to think, plan, and make decisions about their work?

▶ *Practice What You've Learned*

Notes about Preparing Yourself

Use this space to record your thoughts about your personal journey toward becoming a responsive child-centered practitioner.

What new roles would you like to try out?

_____

_____

_____

_____

_____

_____

_____

_____

_____

_____

Is there a disposition you want to enhance or try to replace in yourself?

_____

_____

_____

_____

_____

_____

_____

_____

How can you further cultivate your own sense of aesthetics, wonder, and joy in the world?

_____

_____

_____

_____

_____

_____

_____

_____

Afterword—
Keep It Going!

In today's world, early childhood educators face many challenges but also have many exciting opportunities. No doubt you've discovered some thought-provoking research and resources to support your philosophy and goals for children. You may discover as you move into teaching that the work is very different than what you anticipated. Perhaps you experience more expectations and demands on how you spend your time, leaving little room for the spontaneity and joy that you associate with childhood. Many teachers report they spend more time on managing behaviors than on exciting curriculum projects. Others discover that all the work they've put into planning lessons for children doesn't actually translate into an excitement or hold the children's attention for very long.

In the early part of the twenty-first century, concerns about these challenges dominated the stories we (the authors) were hearing from teachers. We simultaneously noticed that subtle shifts began taking place in our profession's vernacular. Increasingly we now hear the term "early education" replacing "early childhood education." Just as teachers have been telling us, the children themselves seem to be slipping out of the education picture.

Keep Children at the Center

We titled this book *Reflecting Children's Lives,* and in the educational context of this second edition, we offer this phrase as ever more compelling as a guideline for teachers. With all the pressures educators experience, keeping children's lives at the center of your thinking will keep you lively and learning as a teacher. Keeping a close eye on children, not as an act of mistrust, but rather as a commitment to seeing the details of their pursuits, will serve as an antidote to teacher discouragement and burnout. When you reflect children's lives in your planning, you'll discover academic learning becomes meaningful for the children and not merely a nod to meeting standards.

Each chapter in this book offers guidelines and activities to assess your current thinking and practices and provides numerous examples of things to try. In addition to the stories from teachers found here, we have produced a short video, *Children at the Center* (www.ecetrainers.com), in which you see five teachers working with the ideas in this book and hear reflections on the changes they made to keep children at the center. We encourage you to draw inspiration as well as specific ideas from the work of these teachers and other colleagues you seek out to keep you grounded in child-centered practices. We've included e-mail addresses so you really can send the letters we ask you to write to the teachers who generously shared their stories at the end of each chapter. Our hope is to further an ongoing dialogue and support for these practices.

Keep Nourishing and Challenging Yourself

The last chapter of this book suggested different ways to continue developing yourself as a child-centered teacher. This involves not only finding ways to nourish yourself but also continually taking on the challenge of rethinking how you understand your work with children and the teaching and learning process. Before spending money on workshops or conferences, think carefully about your goals.

- How does what this conference offers relate to my professional development goals?

- What knowledge base, skill set, or dispositional learning am I trying to enhance?

- What specific sessions in the conference program should be my priority?

- How could I prepare myself with some advance reading, web searching, or reflective writing?

- What is my specific plan for sharing and implementing what I will learn?

As an alternative to spending your limited professional development dollars on conferences, consider who might provide mentoring for you in the area you are trying to strengthen. Seek out local mentoring programs that may be available in your community, or set up a peer mentoring relationship with someone you know. Consider forming a group that meets monthly to examine your work with children (often referred to as a professional learning community [PLC] or community of practice).

The isolation teachers often experience in their work can limit their learning. Finding another program to visit can generate new ideas and energy. To make this a lasting professional development experience, approach it with the self-assessment and goal-setting process described above. As with attending conferences, it's important to have a clear focus when teachers tour other programs. Otherwise you can slip into a shopping mind-set, trying to find out where to buy cool stuff. While discovering sources for new materials can be beneficial, this is hardly a focus that will sustain professional development. Often you can arrange an independent visit to a program you hope to learn from or become part of a study tour group that typically combines center tours with presentations and reflective discussions with participants. A bit of probing on the Internet can lead to some possible study tour options: you can typically find listings on our website (www.ecetrainers.com) or others, such as Chicago Commons

Child Development Program (www.chicagocommons.org), Child Care Exchange (www.childcareexchange.com), London Bridge Child Care Services (www.londonbridge.com), and the North American Reggio Emilia Alliance (www.reggioalliance.org).

Keep Your Work Worthy of Our Children

Before his passing, one of Tom Hunter's quiet yet persistent calls to action was his song "Worthy of Our Children" (1990). It is one of those easy zipper songs where new phrases are offered as new verses:

> May the work we do
> Make the world we live in
> A little more worthy of our children.
>
> May the _____ _____ _____
> Make the world we live in
> A little more worthy of our children.

This simple song holds great potential for examining our work as early childhood educators. We have all sorts of assessment tools available to us now—and this song is a compelling addition. Consult a thesaurus and you typically find these synonyms for the word *worthy:* fully deserving, commendable, praiseworthy, laudable, admirable, valuable, precious, and creditable.

Each of these words adds a new dimension to assessing your work with children. Review them again. Mentally walk through your family child care home or classroom or an early childhood program that is familiar to you, trying each of these words in your mind's eye: *fully deserving, commendable, praiseworthy, laudable, admirable, valuable, precious, creditable.* Does this place earn these descriptors?

Notice again the sequencing of phrases in Tom's song:

> May the work we do
> Make the world we live in
> A little more worthy of our children.

His call is that our work improves the world. It's not just earning stars on a rating scale or data on test scores. Far too often our entire field settles for mediocrity. There are excuses, gripes, barriers, good reasons to feel like more is not possible. But the teachers we see who rise above just meeting the standards have a strong sense of purpose, philosophical clarity, and values—rather than regulations—guiding their priorities. Instead of "They won't let us . . . ," you hear them say, "How can we figure this out?" Rather than "We can't . . . ," their mantra is "What *can* we do? What next steps can we take?"

To guide your considerations, you could use Tom's song as a provocation. What new verses would you slip in to express your intention to have your work be worthy of our children?

Keep It Going

When he was alive, Tom Hunter's songs, work, and life offered teachers sustenance and inspiration. One of the clearest phrases to come from him in the last days of his life was "Keep it going!" Even as you face challenges, feel weary or frustrated, you can as an educator and children's advocate continue the work of seeing that children's lives are reflected in all our educational policies and practices. We can commit ourselves to making our work and our lives worthy of our children.

> May the *places we create,*
> Make the world we live in,
> A little more worthy of our children.
>
> May the *words we speak,*
> Make the world we live in,
> A little more worthy of our children.
>
> May the *things we plan,*
> Make the world we live in,
> A little more worthy of our children
>
> May the *lives we live,*
> Make the world we live in,
> A little more worthy of our children.

References

Carter, Margie, and Deb Curtis. 1996. *Spreading the News: Sharing the Stories of Early Childhood Education*. Saint Paul, MN: Redleaf Press.

Cronin, Sharon, and Carmen Sosa Massó. 2003. *Soy Bilingüe: Language, Culture, and Young Latino Children*. Seattle: Center for Linguistic and Cultural Democracy. www.culturaldemocracy.org.

Curtis, Deb, and Margie Carter. 2000. *The Art of Awareness: How Observation Can Transform Your Teaching*. Saint Paul, MN: Redleaf Press.

———. 2003. *Designs for Living and Learning: Transforming Early Childhood Environments*. Saint Paul, MN: Redleaf Press.

———. 2008. *Learning Together with Young Children: A Curriculum Framework for Reflective Teachers*. Saint Paul, MN: Redleaf Press.

Graves, Judy, and Susan MacKay. 2009. "One School's Response to State Standards." *Innovations in Early Education* 16 (1): 10.

Hunter, Tom. 1990. "Worthy of Our Children." On *Bits & Pieces*, The Song Growing Company, compact disc. www.tomhunter.com.

———. 2008. "As Human as They Can Be." On *As Human as They Can Be*, The Song Growing Company, DVD. www.tomhunter.com.

Katz, Lilian. 1986. "Current Perspectives on Child Development." *Council for Research in Music Education* 86:1–9.

———. 2008a. "Another Look at What Young Children Should Be Learning." *Exchange* 180 (March–April): 53–56.

———. 2008b. "Academic versus Intellectual Learning." *ExchangeEveryDay*, March 24.

Lally, J. Ronald 1995. "The Impact of Child Care Policies and Practices on Infant/Toddler Identity Formation." *Young Children* 51 (1): 58–67.

Lieberman, Evelyn Jackson. 1985. "Name Writing and the Preschool Child." PhD diss., University of Arizona.

National Geographic Society. 1983. *Peoples and Places of the Past: The National Geographic Illustrated Cultural Atlas of the Ancient World.* Washington, DC: National Geographic Society.

Schirrmacher, Robert, and Jill Englebright Fox. 2008. *Art and Creative Development for Young Children.* 6th ed. Albany, NY: Delmar.

Trook, E. 1983. "Understanding Teachers' Use of Power: A Role-Playing Activity." In *On the Growing Edge: Notes by College Teachers Making Changes,* edited by Elizabeth Jones, 15–22. Pasadena, CA: Pacific Oakes College.

Index